ASTRONOMY

▲ by Liz Kruesi

Content Consultant

David Weintraub
Professor of Astronomy
Vanderbilt University

Essential Library

An Imprint of Abdo Publishing | abdopublishing.com

CUTTING EDGE
SCIENCE +
TECHNOLOGY

abdopublishing.com

Published by Abdo Publishing, a division of ABDO, PO Box 398166, Minneapolis, Minnesota 55439. Copyright © 2016 by Abdo Consulting Group, Inc. International copyrights reserved in all countries. No part of this book may be reproduced in any form without written permission from the publisher. Essential Library™ is a trademark and logo of Abdo Publishing.

Printed in the United States of America, North Mankato, Minnesota
092015
012016

THIS BOOK CONTAINS RECYCLED MATERIALS

Cover Photo: L. Calcada/ESO

Interior Photos: JPL-Caltech/ESO/R. Hurt/NASA, 4-5; JPL-Caltech/NASA, 7; NASA, 8, 13, 15, 33, 41, 44–45, 49, 61, 67, 68–69, 72, 75, 77, 80–81, 88–89; Equinox Graphics/Science Source, 9; David Parker/Science Source, 10; Science Source, 16–17, 96; Royal Astronomical Society/Science Source, 21; Dorling Kindersley/Thinkstock, 22, 23; Bettmann/Corbis, 25; West Wind Graphics/iStockphoto, 26–27; Royal Greenwich Observatory/Science Source, 29; Tatsuo Nakjima/Yomiuri Shimbun/AP Images, 31; Enrico Sacchetti/Science Source, 34–35; Nico Hammer, H.-Th. Janka, Ewald Müller & Markus Rampp/Max-Planck-Institut für Astrophysik/Science Source, 36–37; Jitze Couperus CC2.0, 39; Alexandros Alexakis/Science Source, 43; AP Images, 47; Harvard-Smithsonian Center for Astrophysics/Steffen Richter/VagabondPix.co/Corbis, 51; Rick Friedman/Corbis, 52; G. Gillet/ESO, 53; Ames/JPL-Caltech/NASA, 54–55; Aldaron/Wikimedia Commons, 57; John D. & Catherine T. MacArthur Foundation, 59; Lynette Cook/Science Source, 63; Ben Margot/AP Images, 65; Stefanie Keenan/Women A.R.E./Getty Images, 71; Nikolay Pandev/iStockphoto, 79; SPL/Science Source, 83; James King-Holmes/Science Source, 85; HO/Ariane ESPACE/AP Images, 91; Red Line Editorial, 92–93; Winfried Rothermel/AP Images, 95; European Space Agency/Science Source, 99

Editor: Arnold Ringstad
Series Designer: Craig Hinton

Library of Congress Control Number: 2015945644

Cataloging-in-Publication Data
Kruesi, Liz.
  Astronomy / Liz Kruesi.
    p. cm. -- (Cutting-edge science and technology)
  ISBN 978-1-62403-913-3 (lib. bdg.)
  Includes bibliographical references and index.
  1. Astronomy--Juvenile literature. 2. Solar system--Juvenile literature.   I. Title.
  520--dc23
                                    2015945644

CONTENTS

GOING THE DISTANCE

We live on a planet that, along with seven other planets and countless smaller bodies, orbits the sun. Our sun is one of approximately 200 billion stars in the Milky Way galaxy, and most of those stars appear likely to host planets of their own.[1] Our galaxy is just one island of lights in the universe's vast sea of hundreds of billions of galaxies. Each galaxy is made up of billions of individual stars.

Astronomy is the study of all the objects that make up the universe outside Earth—from the planets and comets in our solar system to the many types of stars in galaxies that are sprinkled across the universe. To learn about these celestial objects, astronomers study them using telescopes and other scientific instruments.

Because current technology makes it impossible to leave the Milky Way, the only images showing the whole galaxy at once are artists' impressions.

Like a Magnifying Glass in Space

Astronomers can use a trick of gravity to find distant galaxies. Anything in the universe that has mass—a galaxy, a star, even a planet—warps the space around it. The biggest cosmic structures, such as clusters of hundreds of galaxies, have so much mass their gravity has a major impact on nearby matter and light. When the light from a distant galaxy passes the galaxy cluster, the light changes direction due to the warped space. If the distant galaxy, the galaxy cluster, and an observer using a telescope all lay along a line, that light is bent just right so it gives the astronomer a magnified view of the distant galaxy. The galaxy cluster acts like a giant magnifying glass in space. These alignments make it possible for astronomers to find many distant galaxies and stars.

A telescope is a time machine. The light it collects from objects in space has a specific speed limit. Light cannot travel faster than 186,282 miles per second (299,792 kms).[2] That means when an astronomer uses a telescope to observe a distant galaxy, she studies light that has taken a long time to travel to Earth.

Astronomers measure a distance in space by how long light takes to travel that distance. One light-year is the distance light travels in one Earth year. It is approximately 5.9 trillion miles (9.5 trillion km). The nearest large galaxy to ours is the Andromeda Galaxy. It is 2.5 million light years away.[3] This means when astronomers turn a telescope to this galaxy, visible from the Northern Hemisphere, they see light that left Andromeda approximately 2.5 million years ago. The scale of our solar system is much smaller. The moon is approximately 1.3 light seconds away, and the sun is approximately eight light minutes away. The most distant planet, Neptune, is approximately four light hours from the sun.

Some scientists study nearby galaxies such as Andromeda, but others research the more distant galaxies that lie much farther from Earth. The light that left these galaxies has been traveling for

Modern astronomers see Andromeda as it appeared 2.5 million years ago, when humans were first evolving on Earth.

The gravity of distant objects can distort and magnify light, creating a gravitational lens. The result can be a circular ring of light around a celestial object, right.

billions of years. Our universe is now approximately 13.8 billion years old.[4] These very distant galaxies formed in the universe's first 1 billion years. Astronomers are looking for the first galaxies that lit up our cosmos. Every year, they break their distance records. New technology lets them collect older light.

Look to the Light

Light is astronomy's crucial messenger. Many types of light exist, and each kind has a certain energy depending on its wavelength. To visualize what wavelength is, imagine two people holding a string loosely between them. One person starts moving his arm up and down to create a wave. The distance from one peak of the string's wave to the next peak is the wave's wavelength. Light's wavelength dictates what type of light it is.

The kind of light human eyes can see ranges from red light to violet. The colors vary based on wavelength. But beyond the narrow band of wavelengths we can see, light also comes in forms we cannot see. All types of light fall along what is called the electromagnetic spectrum.

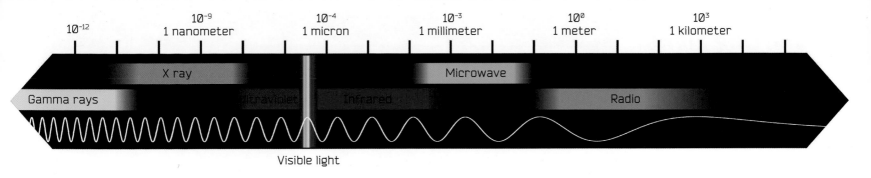

Visible light

Visible light only occupies a narrow sliver of the electromagnetic spectrum.

How do the wavelengths of different types of light compare? Red has a longer wavelength than violet. Infrared light has a longer wavelength than red light. Microwaves and radio waves have even longer wavelengths. Longer-wavelength light carries less energy than shorter-wavelength light.

Several types of light have shorter wavelengths than we can see with the naked eye. Ultraviolet light, X rays, and gamma rays are all included in this group. These types of light carry a great deal of energy. They are often associated with high-energy events in space, such as massive explosions. Astronomers have developed tools to observe many different wavelengths of light in space.

Spying Light from Galaxies

The light from galaxies reveals their distances. To study a galaxy, astronomers examine its light in many wavelengths. If that galaxy appears to be moving toward Earth, astronomers see its light get a bit bluer in color. Its light is shifted to smaller wavelengths. If the galaxy appears to be moving away from us, the light is a bit redder. It has longer wavelengths. These color changes happen for the same reason you hear a slightly higher pitched sound from a train or ambulance coming toward you than you do when it is moving away. This phenomenon is called the Doppler effect.

Shifting Light

Top: To an observer on Earth, a galaxy that appears to be stationary with relation to Earth will have its light at the expected region of the electromagnetic spectrum.

Middle: To an observer on Earth, a galaxy that appears to be moving away from Earth will have its light pushed toward the red end of the spectrum.

Bottom: To an observer on Earth, a galaxy that appears to be moving toward Earth will have its light pushed toward the blue end of the spectrum.

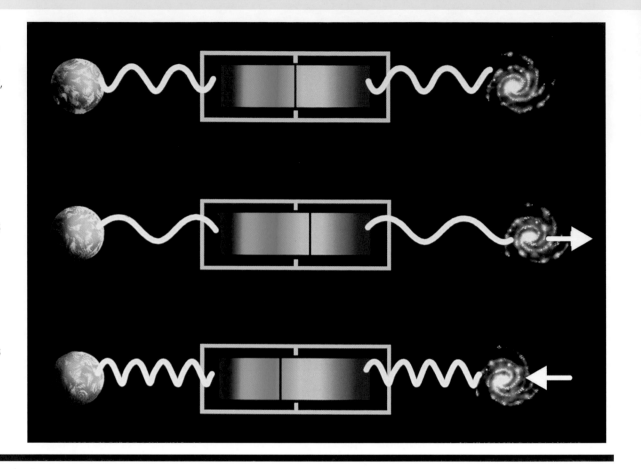

When astronomers look at a galaxy, they look for these kinds of patterns in the light. They can determine how fast the galaxy appears to be speeding toward or away from us. In reality, the space between galaxies is being stretched, rather than the galaxies themselves moving through space.

When astronomers look at all the wavelengths of light the stars in a galaxy give off, they see some colors that are special. Specific elements give off certain colors of light. For instance, atoms of hydrogen, the most common element in the universe, emit violet, aqua, and red light. Scientists can study these colors to determine what elements make up faraway celestial objects.

Astronomers have discovered our universe is expanding over time. As it grows bigger, galaxies move farther away from one another. The expansion also stretches the light from those galaxies. So even though the hydrogen in a far-away galaxy gives off the violet, aqua, and red colors, the expansion of space has stretched that light. Each color is shifted toward the red end of the spectrum. Light also tells astronomers how far away a galaxy is.

In May 2015, astronomers found light that left a galaxy when it was just 570 million years old.[5] That light has been traveling for 13.1 billion years. This galaxy is moving away from us very fast, and it now lies very far away. This galaxy, named EGS-zs8-1, became the oldest and most distant galaxy astronomers had found yet.

Find the First Ones

The continuing search for the oldest and most distant galaxies is a direct result of improvements in telescope technology. Larger telescopes can see fainter objects. This is because they have larger

Distant Record Holders

Astronomers have found thousands of planets orbiting other stars. Most are within a few thousand light years of Earth. However, two known exoplanets are approximately 27,000 light-years from Earth.[6] Most stars astronomers can see lie in our Milky Way galaxy. The most distant star they have found in our galaxy lies approximately 890,000 light-years from us. It is in the galaxy's dim outskirts.[7]

A few stars explode at the end of their lives, resulting in a supernova. This explosion disperses material into space. These blasts are very bright, and astronomers can see them from far away. The most distant supernova they have found so far exploded more than 10 billion years ago.[8]

surface areas to collect more light, just as a larger bucket would collect more rainwater.

Astronomers found hints of EGS-zs8-1 in photos from the Hubble Space Telescope, an observatory orbiting Earth. Hubble's main mirror is 7.9 feet (2.4 m) across.[9] But to look at the infrared light and confirm the galaxy's distance, they used a huge telescope in Hawaii. It collects light using a mirror 33 feet (10 m) across![10]

A space telescope planned for a 2018 launch will be able to see even older galaxies. The James Webb Space Telescope (JWST) will detect the infrared light from the earliest galaxies. It will also be bigger than Hubble, at 21 feet (6.5m) across.[11] Because it will fly far above our planet's atmosphere, the JWST will have a clearer view into space than telescopes on Earth's surface. Astronomers say it will be able to see the earliest stars and galaxies as they were just starting to light up. This telescope will be able to see back to the universe's first 200 million years.[12]

Hubble's deepest views into space show galaxies more than 13 billion years old.

The Awesome Universe

Astronomers are discovering many exciting things about our universe, in addition to some of the first galaxies that formed. They have found thousands of exoplanets. They have learned giant black holes

Galactic Shapes

The galaxies of the universe have many shapes, colors, and sizes. Our Milky Way galaxy is a large, complex galaxy. Clumps of gas and dust trace spiral arms that extend from the ends of a dense, bright bar at the center. At the center of our galaxy is an enormous black hole, an invisible object that attracts any matter and light that approach too closely.

The universe's early galaxies had less complicated structures. The galaxies that lived in the universe's first billion years were much smaller than most of the galaxies that exist now. They contained clouds of gas and clumps of thousands of stars.

live at the center of every large galaxy. And they have discovered some massive stars become the strongest magnets you could imaginable.

Astronomers also know everything we see—all of these galaxies, stars, and planets—make up only 4.9 percent of the cosmos. The other 95.1 percent is completely invisible.[16] The telescopes and other scientific instruments being built today will help tomorrow's astronomers solve the mysteries of the universe.

Scientists have spent years testing the mirrors and other parts of the $8 billion JWST.

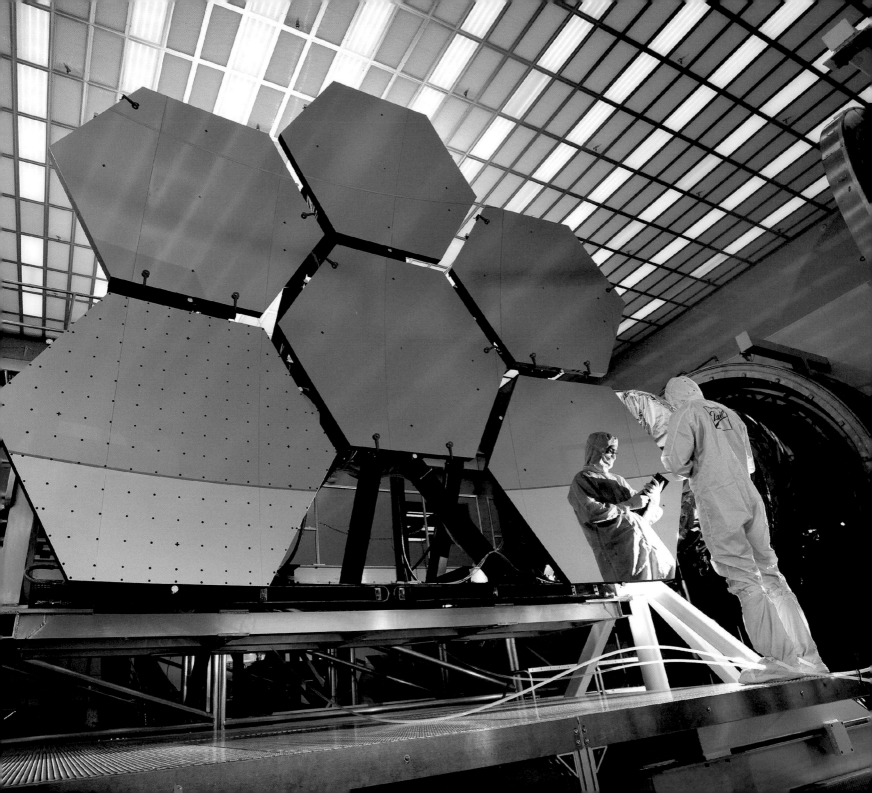

TWO

BEGINNING A COSMIC EXPLORATION

Ancient people looked into the night sky and saw distinct points of light, fuzzy stars, and milky clouds. It took advanced technology to determine the true nature of these objects. The first clues were revealed more than 400 years ago, when Italian scientist Galileo Galilei turned one of the first telescopes to the hazy Milky Way band that sweeps across the night sky.

His instrument magnified his view by 20 times, showing him the Milky Way arc and other hazy regions were made of up many individual points of light, each one a star.[1] Suddenly the known universe looked a lot bigger.

Galileo's ideas ran counter to religious beliefs that suggested Earth was at the center of the universe.

Late in the 1700s, British astronomer William Herschel used a telescope that could magnify the sky by

▲Telescope Inventor

Although many people credit Italian Galileo Galilei with inventing the telescope, he was not the first to use the tool. Historians believe Dutch inventor Hans Lippershey first aligned lenses in a tube to magnify distant objects. This new invention was revealed in the Netherlands in October 1608, several months before Galileo used one.

nearly 160 times. He spent more than a year counting the number of stars in different regions of the sky. He determined the Milky Way is shaped like a thick disk filled with millions of stars. Herschel realized more stars were located near the center of the disk than at the outskirts. Over the next few decades, he also found more than 2,500 nebulae. These objects get their name from the Latin word for clouds. They were blurry clouds of light, and astronomers did not know what they could be.

Nearly every one of those clouds, as it turned out, is a galaxy. Centuries of discoveries have continued to show just how huge our universe is. They have revealed the wide variety of objects our cosmos holds.

See the Rainbow

To learn about the universe, scientists use advanced prisms to spread apart the light coming from objects. Researchers in the latter half of the 1800s realized when they did this, the spread-out light had black lines in it, as if some of the colors were missing. Each chemical element absorbs or emits certain colors when viewed this way, so light can reveal the composition of objects at a distance. The researchers had discovered the elements' signatures of light.

In the 1910s, American astronomer Vesto Slipher spread out the light of more than a dozen starry clouds, looking for missing colors. He saw the dark lines were not at the expected colors, but instead had shifted to redder colors. The light shift Slipher found showed how fast each of those objects was moving—and they were receding from Earth.

Variable Stars

All stars do not send out the same amount of light. If they did, astronomers could easily figure out the distance to any star in the universe by measuring how bright it appears and comparing that value to how much light they would know it sends out. But a special type of star found in the early 1780s and first understood in the early 1900s gave scientists a way to calculate distances that is equally effective. It is known as a Cepheid variable star.

This kind of star changes in brightness due to its sloshing insides. By 1908 astronomer Henrietta Swan Leavitt found more than 1,700 of these special stars and compared how long it took for the stars to go through a full cycle from brightest to faintest and back to brightest.[2] When she plotted the stars on a graph, comparing the brightness and the time it took to go through the cycle, she discovered a relationship. Slower changes happen in brighter stars, while faster changes happen in fainter stars.

This discovery means an astronomer who watches one of these special changing stars and measures how fast the changes occur can figure out how much energy that star is sending out. Then, by comparing how much light is collected to how much energy the star sends out, the astronomer can calculate how far away the star is.

Charting the Galaxies

US astronomer Edwin Hubble used this technique to make one of the most important discoveries in the history of science. He had help from a brand new telescope with a mirror spanning 100 inches (254 cm) atop a mountain in southern California.[3]

In 1923, Hubble found one of Leavitt's variable stars in a large cloudy patch of stars, the Andromeda Nebula. He watched how that star changed in brightness over the next few months and determined it was approximately 1 million light-years away.[4] However, observations showed the Milky Way was only approximately one-tenth that size. Hubble had shown Andromeda is an entirely separate galaxy. This suggested the universe might be filled with billions of individual galaxies. Astronomers using more precise modern techniques later found the Andromeda Galaxy lies approximately 2.5 million light-years from us.[5]

Hubble's work was not yet complete. He and fellow astronomer Milton Humason chose two dozen newly discovered galaxies to study in depth. They looked at how much the light had been shifted toward the red, which told them how fast those galaxies were speeding away from Earth. Then, using different measurements and techniques, they estimated distances to those same galaxies.

Galaxies farther away from us are moving away from us faster. This relationship is now known as Hubble's law. The discovery made it clear the universe is expanding.

LENSES OR MIRRORS?

Telescopes collect light from an object and guide the light to the observer, camera, or other detector. The first telescopes used lenses. These pieces of glass bend the incoming light and focus it to one point. The problem with a lens is that it bends light of different colors differently. Red is bent less than purple. This issue is apparent when astronomers use large telescopes that require thick glass lenses.

So instead, scientists prefer to use mirrors, which produce more accurate images. The first telescopes that used mirrors instead of lenses to send the light down the telescope tube were introduced in the 1660s. English scientist Isaac Newton, who also made great advances in mathematics and physics, invented one of the earliest mirror-based designs.

» Telescopes with lenses refract, or bend, the light that enters them. This can distort the light. Additionally, large lenses are expensive and difficult to build.

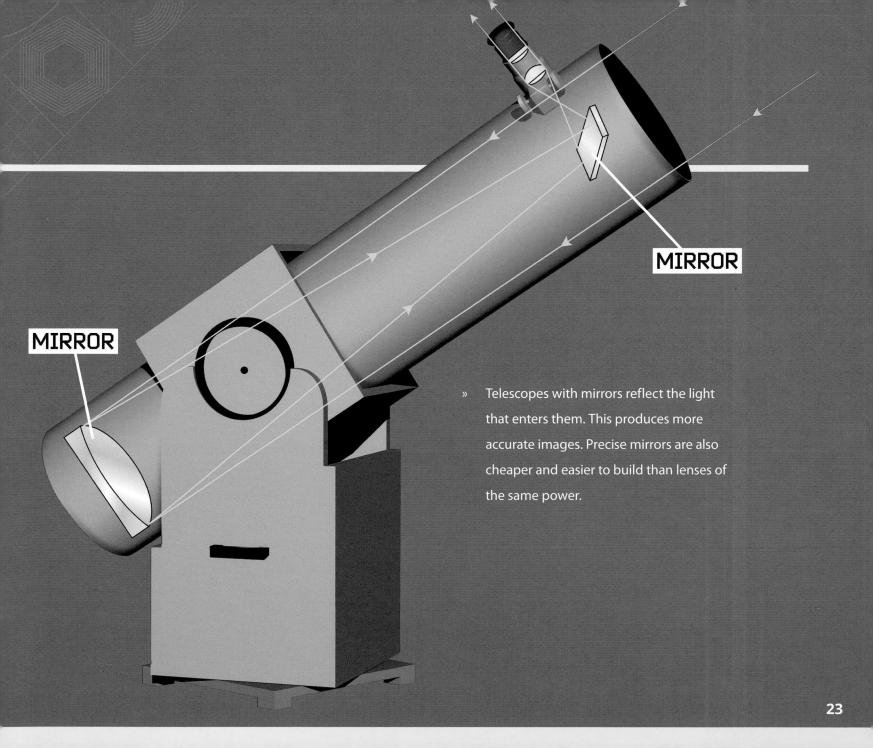

MIRROR

MIRROR

» Telescopes with mirrors reflect the light that enters them. This produces more accurate images. Precise mirrors are also cheaper and easier to build than lenses of the same power.

The decades that have passed since these discoveries were made have brought about many technologically advanced tools astronomers can use to observe the light from the cosmos. Sophisticated computer programs make it possible to quickly analyze vast amounts of data. Many questions have been answered, but new tools and techniques have also led to new questions. Today's astronomers are performing cutting-edge research to find the answers.

Hubble's discoveries showed the universe is dramatically larger than people had previously thought.

THREE

THE TOOLS OF
ASTRONOMY

Telescopes have been important tools for observing the universe over the past four centuries. They use mirrors and lenses to force light on a path leading to a detector. At the advent of telescopes, that detector was the human eye. When photography technology emerged in the mid-1800s, scientists placed early cameras at the eyepieces of telescopes. Today's astronomers use various types of digital cameras and other detectors. Some collect visible light to create an image. Some detectors make observations in infrared, radio wave, or X-ray areas of the electromagnetic spectrum. Others, called spectrometers, collect the light and spread it out to see the colors emitted by the target object.

Many of the largest ground-based telescopes, including the Keck telescopes on Mauna Kea in Hawaii, are built atop mountains.

Astronomers strive for larger telescopes and more sensitive detectors. A bigger surface area will guide more light to the detector, and a more sensitive detector will capture more details of the observed target. These instruments have evolved rapidly in the past few decades, leading to incredible observations. Astronomers have seen solar systems forming around distant stars and clumps of young stars hidden in the arms of galaxies.

The instruments of astronomy permit scientists to study the cosmos across all types of light. Observations are made from the surface of Earth, atop some of the highest mountains, aboard planes and balloons, and in space. Some instruments orbit Earth, and some drift through space far from their home planet.

Multiple Mirrors

Today's most advanced ground-based telescopes have circular mirrors between 26 and 34 feet (7.9 and 10.4 m) wide. The best way to build these huge mirrors is by combining multiple smaller ones. Many of today's largest optical telescopes use this technique, including Hawaii's twin Keck telescopes, the South African Large Telescope, and Gran Telescopio Canarias on the Canary Islands off the coast of northwest Africa.

To collect light and focus it into a detailed picture, the mirror needs to be extremely smooth. Bumps on the surface must be smaller than the wavelength of light they are observing. Otherwise,

Telescope mirrors undergo extreme polishing to make them smooth.

they will bounce the light in the wrong direction. Visible light has a wavelength of approximately half a millionth of a meter. That is only few thousand times the size of an atom.

Scientists have just begun building the next generation of telescopes, which will be even larger. They will span up to 128 feet (39 m) in diameter, and they will get their first glimpses of light in the next decade.[3] Two of these huge instruments, the Giant Magellan Telescope (GMT) and the European Extremely Large Telescope (E-ELT), will study the southern sky from Chile. A third, the Thirty Meter Telescope (TMT), will observe the northern sky from Hawaii.

The GMT will have seven mirrors 27.5 feet (8.4 m) wide, each polished to a smoothness of approximately 20 billionths of a meter. If one of these mirrors were the size of the continental United States, the largest bumps would be no taller than one-half inch (1.3 cm).[4] Both the TMT and E-ELT will need to be just as smooth to accurately collect light and focus it into detailed images.

◢ Quiet Zones

Radio telescopes need quiet zones. However, this does not mean you cannot speak around the telescopes. Instead, you cannot use television and cell phones. The electromagnetic waves these devices emit are in the same range as radio telescopes, so they can interfere with the telescopes' operation. Some very sensitive telescopes can even be thrown off by other small electronic devices. At an observatory in Virginia, scientists struggled to figure out why their data seemed off. They finally realized the culprit was the battery-operated fans sold in the observatory's gift shop.

Working Together

Astronomers can use computers to combine the signals from smaller telescopes into one image. This type of setup, known as an array, is common in radio astronomy. Radio signals have long wavelengths, ranging from a hundredth of an inch to hundreds of feet. Scientists can use radio dishes or even antennae to collect these waves. The advanced Atacama Large Millimeter/submillimeter Array (ALMA) in Chile began making observations in 2011. It has 66 separate radio

Each of ALMA's dozens of radio dishes dwarfs the array's human operators.

dishes working as one. Astronomers can move them around to create the equivalent of a telescope ten miles (16 km) wide.[5]

A radio array still in the planning stages, called the Square Kilometre Array, will have telescope setups at two separate locations on Earth. They will make observations together as one instrument, effectively creating a single enormous radio telescope. Plans call for approximately 200 dishes in South Africa and approximately 130,000 antennae, which are each much less expensive to build, in Australia.[6] Astronomers are testing the technology on smaller scales at these locations.

Above the Atmosphere

Earth has a thick atmosphere that is crucial for life on our planet. It absorbs harmful radiation and high-speed particles from the sun and elsewhere in space, blocking them from reaching life on the surface. But this protective atmosphere also complicates astronomy. It keeps many wavelengths of light from the view of the telescopes on Earth's surface.

Visible light makes it to the ground, and some colors of infrared light and most radio waves also pass through the atmosphere. Both of these types of light have less energy than visible light.

But radiation that has more energy—the types of radiation that carry information about exploding stars, black holes, and forming stars—cannot pass through the atmosphere. To look at these types of light, astronomers must use detectors outside Earth's atmosphere.

The Highest Energy

Astronomers have been sending X-ray telescopes and detectors above the atmosphere since the 1960s. X rays have much more energy than visible light, so an X ray would pass right through an ordinary telescope's mirror. Astronomers use nested, concentric cylinders with mirrored coatings to guide the X rays at shallow angles toward the detector and other instruments. NASA's most recent X-ray telescope, called NuSTAR, has 133 concentric mirrors.[7]

To study gamma rays, which have even higher energies than X rays, scientists use other types of detectors. They measure the energy and direction of each incoming gamma ray. These do not create

pictures in the way visible-light detectors do. They generate maps showing where the highest-energy gamma rays come from.

Advancing Astronomy's Sight

Nearly everything astronomers know about the universe comes from light they collect with various types of telescopes. Because no single observatory can detect all wavelengths, astronomers often study the same object with different telescopes that specialize in particular types of light.

These devices have evolved greatly since they were first used. Scientists now focus on two types of studies that complement each other. The first is exploring fine details in single objects. The second is carrying out surveys of big areas of the sky. Combining these two methods gives astronomers information about the behavior of individual stars and of the universe as a whole.

ADAPTIVE OPTICS

Earth's atmosphere distorts incoming light, which is why stars twinkle in the night sky. This effect makes stars, galaxies, and any other objects seen through a telescope appear bigger and warped.

Astronomers, though, can use a technique known as adaptive optics to precisely adjust a telescope's mirrors to offset these effects. "If you think about the atmosphere as introducing something like a circus fun house mirror that distorts how you look," says astronomer Andrea Ghez, "the job of adaptive optics is to introduce a second fun house mirror that undoes the effects [and makes] you look normal again."[11]

Today's biggest and best telescopes, including those at Hawaii's Keck Observatory, where Ghez works, have tiny motors on the back of a bendable secondary mirror. The telescope uses a bright star in the sky as a guide. A computer program knows the star should be a point of light instead of blurry, so it calculates how each mirror needs to bend for that star to look like a single point. The motors push and pull to change the mirrors' shapes. The system repeats this analysis thousands of times each second.

THE KECK TELESCOPES USE LASERS TO CALIBRATE THEIR ADAPTIVE OPTICS SYSTEMS.

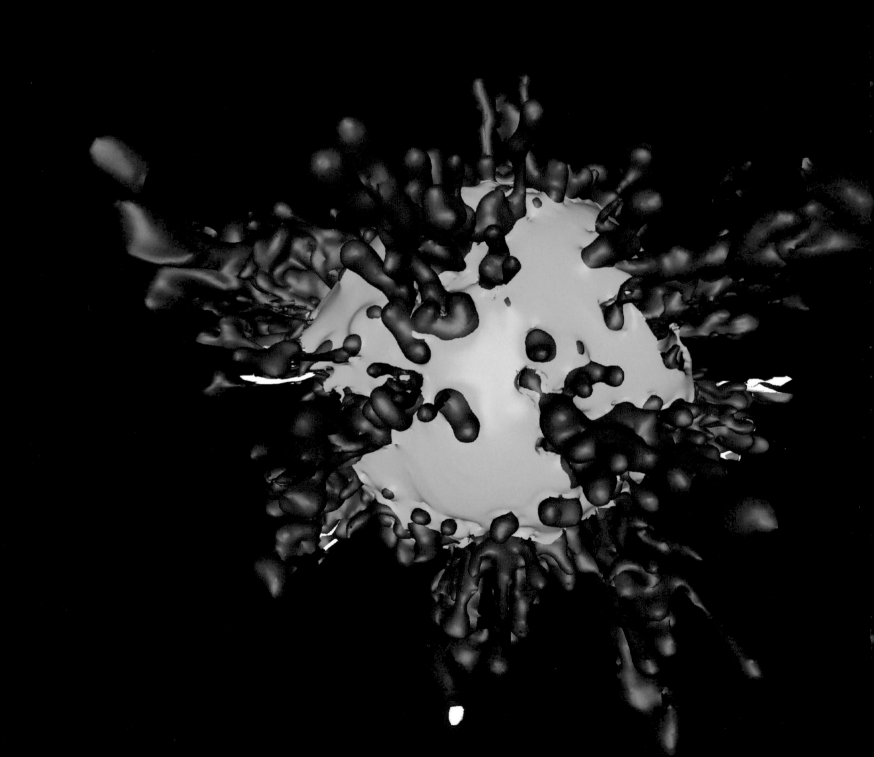

FOUR

SIMULATING THE
UNIVERSE

Studying the light collected by telescopes is one way astronomers learn about our universe. But astronomy occurs on enormous scales. Solar systems span billions of miles, and galaxies take billions of years to form and evolve. Humans can watch only a tiny window of our universe's growth, and they can see only a small portion of what it holds.

To fill in the gaps, scientists rely on their knowledge of physics and their ability to harness the power of computers. Advanced computers are important tools for astronomy research.

Astronomers want to know how the centers of stars burn fuel and release light. They seek to discover how black holes affect light that passes too close. And they are trying to piece together how the planets in our solar system formed. The laws of physics help them understand possible answers to these mysteries. These laws can be expressed in mathematical equations.

Computer models simulate complex events, such as the explosions of stars.

The First Computer

Iowa State College physics professor John Atanasoff built the first electronic computer with graduate student Clifford Berry between 1939 and 1942. Atanasoff came up with the idea in 1937, when he found his calculations were too complex for just pen and paper. A reconstruction of the Atanasoff–Berry Computer is on display at the Computer History Museum in Mountain View, California.

An astronomy computer model takes these equations for the laws of physics and some starting information—such as the star's mass and chemical makeup—and solves the equations. To find how things are expected to change over time, the computer repeats the calculations multiple times. The accuracy of these predictions depends on how good the initial data is and how complete the equations are.

The CDC 6600 was thousands of times slower than modern smartphones.

Scientists use computer models to study phenomena they cannot otherwise see. They use models to have a better idea of what to look for in space. They use models to give possible explanations for unexpected findings in their telescope data. Models also make it possible to sort through the huge amount of observations today's telescopes collect.

Scientists use some of the most powerful supercomputers to run their simulations. The first supercomputer entered use in 1964. Designed by Seymour Cray, the CDC 6600 could perform 3 million calculations every second.[1]

Processing power has improved dramatically over time. The most powerful modern supercomputers can run quadrillions of calculations in a second.[2] These machines are usually made of thousands of computer processors joined together.

Enormous Hauls of Data

As astronomy's detectors record bigger images and more information, scientists receive huge amounts of data to sort through. One of the most advanced cameras used today is the Dark Energy Camera, attached to a telescope 13 feet (4 m) wide in Chile.[3] It can take hundreds of images, generating approximately 400 gigabytes of information, per night. The data is sent to a supercomputer in Illinois. There, a computer program written by researchers pieces together the images into a large mosaic, identifies stars and galaxies, and measures the brightness of each object. Astronomers then analyze this information with other computer programs. One program might look for moving points of light that could be asteroids. Another program could look for stars that suddenly increase in brightness, which may indicate they are exploding.

Future telescopes will collect even more data. The Large Synoptic Survey Telescope (LSST), under construction in Chile, is scheduled to begin observing in 2021. Each 3.2-gigapixel image it takes will cover 49 times the area of the full moon.[4] It will make hundreds or thousands of images each night and map half the sky over just three days. Scientists say the LSST will collect 20 to 30 terabytes of data every single night.[5]

NASA's Pleiades supercomputer consists of thousands of high-speed processors linked together.

Computing the Future

Long gone are the days when an astronomer would put his eye to a telescope and watch for changes in the sky. Instead, computers have taken over this part of astronomical research.

Astronomers use collections of advanced computers to simulate how celestial objects and even the universe as a whole grow and evolve. This field of science probes the largest time scales and the biggest structures known. These places and times are out of the reach of human beings. But using the

◢ Simulating Structure

One area of astronomy research where supercomputers are necessary is the study of how the universe's structure evolved. The research looks into how elements bunch together to create the stars and galaxies that make up today's universe. The simulations from just a decade ago could simulate only a few factors, such as gravity. But today's most advanced simulations incorporate heat, magnetism, and pressure. One such project, called Illustris, followed approximately 12 billion particles over a simulated 13 billion years.[6] The calculations took months to complete.

mathematical laws of physics, scientists can study them in computers.

Scientists rely on computers to sort through the enormous amount of information that telescopes' detectors capture. Astronomers today must have at least basic coding skills, allowing them to write computer programs to search data for the types of objects they are studying. Computers have progressed at an extremely fast pace, and upcoming astronomy projects continue to demand the latest computing technology.

Computer models can be used to study phenomena that are difficult or impossible to observe directly, such as waves on the surface of a star.

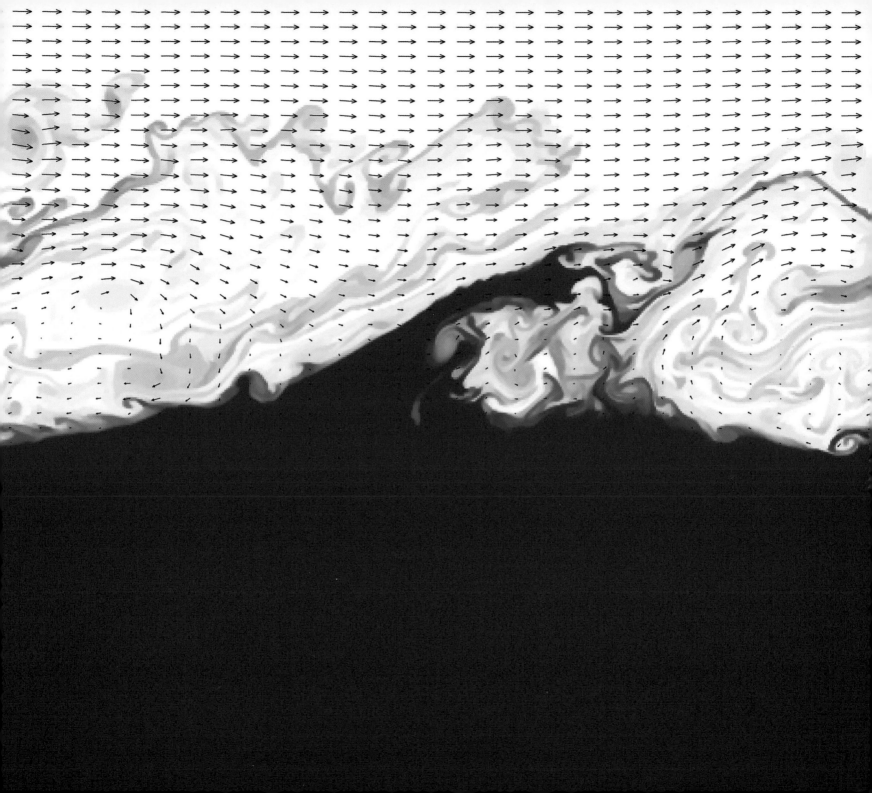

FIVE

THE UNIVERSE'S
BEGINNING

Scientists know the universe is approximately 13.8 billion years old.[1] How close to the birth of the universe—an event known as the big bang—can astronomers study? Telescopes reveal light from a few hundred thousand years after the universe began, which means this light is from the first 0.0028 percent of the universe's age. If the universe was on a human time scale, astronomers would be seeing images of it as a one-month-old infant.

This early cosmic glow shows astronomers what the universe looked like at that young age but also hints at how it changed over time. Scientists have used many telescopes, other instruments, and computer models to learn the universe was once a very compressed, hot, and tiny place. All of the stars, planets, and galaxies in existence today had not yet formed. Instead, great masses of subatomic particles, including protons, electrons, and neutrons, existed in a massive stew.

Many NASA missions have collected data on the big bang.

Some patches of this mixture had a bit more material, while others had a bit less. Over the following millions and billions of years, gravity pulled more material into the denser spots, creating the groups of galaxies that fill our universe today.

Light bounced among the particle stew like balls in a pinball machine. As this collection of matter and energy expanded, its temperature cooled. After approximately 380,000 years, the temperature was cool enough for each proton to grab onto an electron, creating hydrogen atoms. That meant the light had fewer scattered particles to bounce off, and it could finally move freely. Over time, the expansion of the cosmos has lengthened that light into microwaves. This free-moving light carries the earliest pictures of the young universe.

A Glow in Every Direction

Astronomers often make use of the relationship between an object's temperature and the light it emits. Hotter objects give off high-energy light, such as X rays and ultraviolet light. Cooler objects give off low-energy light, such as infrared and microwaves.

In the 1960s, using a radio telescope in New Jersey, American scientists Arno Penzias and Robert Wilson found a microwave signal in every direction they looked. No matter what they did, they could not get rid of this signal. They checked to see if it was coming from nearby New York City, New York, stars in our galaxy, or Earth's atmosphere. They checked their large radio antenna, in case a flaw in the instrument caused the signal. They even scraped off the droppings from pigeons that had been resting inside the antenna. They wanted to eliminate every possible earthly source of the signal.

Around the same time, astronomers at nearby Princeton University had calculated that today's sky should glow in faint microwaves left over from an early, hot universe. They expected the leftover glow

would correspond to a temperature of approximately 5.4 degrees Fahrenheit (3°C) above absolute zero, the coldest possible temperature.[2] This cosmic microwave background (CMB) radiation, as it is called, was exactly what Penzias and Wilson had found.

More advanced instruments over the past five decades have revealed incredible detail in this light. The most recent microwave space observatory, Europe's *Planck* spacecraft, has generated detailed maps of the tiny temperature differences in the CMB.

Maps of the CMB show the extremely slight temperature differences in the early universe. Red areas are warmer than average, and blue areas are cooler than average.

Seeing Patterns

The CMB light may hold additional patterns even today's best instruments strain to see. These are twists in the light, and their signals are incredibly subtle. By studying these tiny twisting patterns, if they exist, astronomers may be able to look back to a time much earlier than the CMB glow: one trillionth of a trillionth of a trillionth of a second after the big bang.[3]

Astronomers think that right after the big bang, the universe expanded tremendously fast. A speck smaller than an atom grew to the size of a softball in a tiny fraction of a second. This era in the universe's history is something scientists can only study using math and computers. They have not yet

been able to see any signals from this time period, known as the inflationary era. The force of this expansion, scientists think, would have thrown waves through the baby universe. These waves, though, are not a type of light. Instead, they are waves of gravity, squishing and stretching space as they move. It is these gravity waves astronomers think imprinted a twisting pattern into the CMB.

Astronomers need incredibly good telescopes to see these patterns. A few such instruments have been looking through the clear skies of Chile and Antarctica. The still, dry air at these locations means the microwaves can travel through mostly unhindered. Astronomers are looking through their data, hoping to find signs of these patterns. If they do not find any, the next step may be to send a telescope into space to search for them.

First Light

Once the first hydrogen atoms absorbed all the light, the early universe went dark. Astronomers think approximately 100 million years later, enough gas had collected to ignite the first stars. These behemoths burned through their material fast, glowing for just a few million years. But during their lives, they combined hydrogen into other chemical elements. When their lives were over, they exploded and threw those elements into space—including carbon, oxygen, and potassium, which are needed for life. The next round of stars and the first galaxies formed millions of years later. As these early stars and galaxies glowed, they burned away a dark cosmic fog, eventually bathing the universe in starlight.

At least, that is what astronomers think happened in the first billion years of our universe. They have not seen the first galaxies or the first stars. Nor have they seen the fog burning away.

Abraham **Loeb**

(1962–)

Imaginative ideas are Harvard University astrophysicist Abraham Loeb's specialty. He spends his days trying to answer unique puzzles in our universe. How can astronomers see the dawn of the stars and galaxies, and how did those objects affect their environments? The early universe is his specialty, but Loeb has also worked on ways to find planets around other stars.

Loeb grew up on his family's farm in Israel. He studied physics at the Hebrew University of Jerusalem, graduating with his PhD in 1986 at the age of 24. After several years at Princeton University, he moved to Harvard in 1993. He says astronomy lets him study the biggest philosophical questions from a scientific perspective.

Several major telescopes on Chilean mountaintops are operated by the European Southern Observatory.

If calculations from Harvard University's Abraham Loeb and his colleagues are correct, radio telescopes that have just started to study the sky might be sensitive enough to see the fog. So, while astronomers might never be able to find the very first lights, they should be able to see how those lights burned lasting signals into cosmic gas.

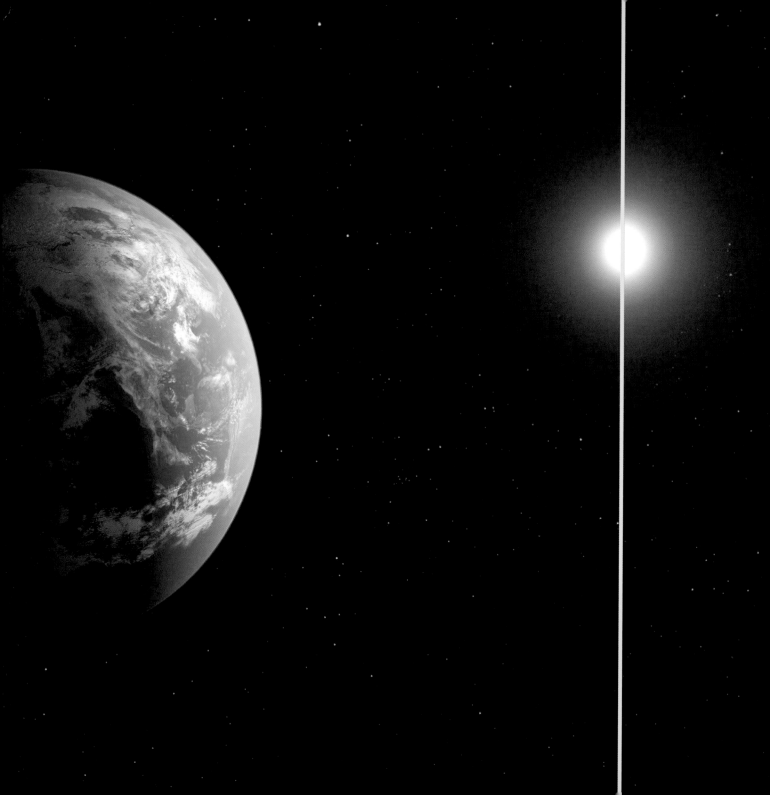

SIX

PLANETS AROUND
OTHER STARS

ur solar system includes eight major planets, but this is only a tiny fraction of the known worlds in the universe. Scientists have found more than 1,500 planets orbiting other stars, and more than 4,000 potential planet discoveries are waiting to be confirmed.[1] These discoveries began trickling in during the 1990s, but it took the technology of the early 2000s to create a revolution.

At first, exoplanet discoveries tended to be of worlds very different from what lay in our solar system. Early discoveries in the 1990s included two worlds found orbiting the dead cinder of a once-massive star and an exoplanet more massive than Jupiter circling its star in just a matter of days. Scientists have since found many surprises, such as an exoplanet orbiting twin stars. But they have also found a star with seven planets of varying sizes, similar to the arrangement of our own solar system. Researchers have not yet found an Earth

An artist's depiction compares Earth, left, to exoplanet Kepler-452b.

twin, but discoveries over time have become more and more similar to our home planet.

The Game Changer

The Kepler space telescope, launched in March 2009, has been instrumental in exoplanet research. It is responsible for finding more than half of the verified exoplanets.

The mission operated for approximately four years and stared at more than 150,000 stars continuously.[2] It was looking for tiny dips in brightness caused by planets passing in front of stars and blocking some of their light. This is known as the transit method. Because Kepler watched the same stars for years, it could detect the brightness dip once for each orbit the planet completed around its star. Such a signal from our solar system would show a dip from Earth once per 365 days, a dip from Mars once per 687 days, and a dip from Venus once per 225 days.[3]

Even though Kepler's aiming system broke down in 2013, astronomers are still working through the huge amounts of data it collected. They continue uncovering more planets. So far, they have found hundreds of worlds that may be similar to Earth in size.

Scientists used Kepler to discover thousands of exoplanets using the transit method. They have found others using a different method. In this technique, they watch how the exoplanet's gravity pulls

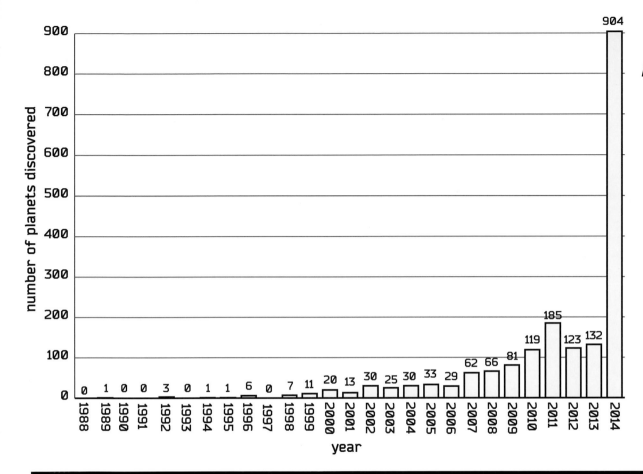

number of planets discovered

900
800
700
600
500
400
300
200
100
0

year	value
1988	0
1989	1
1990	0
1991	0
1992	3
1993	0
1994	1
1995	1
1996	6
1997	0
1998	7
1999	11
2000	20
2001	13
2002	30
2003	25
2004	30
2005	33
2006	29
2007	62
2008	66
2009	81
2010	119
2011	185
2012	123
2013	132
2014	904

year

Exoplanets Discovered by Year

The number of exoplanets discovered has jumped dramatically in recent years thanks to the Kepler space telescope.

on its parent star. They measure tiny changes in the light from the star. The light becomes slightly bluer or slightly redder depending on where the exoplanet is in its orbit. Researchers can learn from these observations what the mass of the planet is, how far it is from the star it orbits, and the duration of its orbit.

◂ A Revived Kepler

In spring 2013, Kepler lost the use of vital control systems and could no longer remain stable enough to stare at the same patch of sky. But just a few months later, scientists showed impressive problem-solving skills and found a different way for the telescope to operate. It now uses the pressure of radiation from the sun to keep it in balance. Scientists dubbed its new mission K2. In its new configuration, Kepler looks at a different patch of the sky every three months. So far, astronomers involved with K2 have uncovered more exoplanets, studied objects within our solar system, and examined black holes in the galaxy.

Needle in a Haystack

Directly detecting exoplanets is extremely difficult. A star may be just a few pixels across in a digital image, but a planet can be a hundred times smaller. Another issue with detecting these planets is brightness. A planet's star far outshines the planet itself. For example, the sun is 10 billion times brighter than Earth.[6] If a telescope looked at our system from 33 light-years away, it would not be able to separate Earth's faint point of light from the much brighter star. The two would appear to lie just 1/36,000th of a degree away from each other.[7]

Right now, the best chance astronomers have to photograph exoplanets is by looking at systems that are only a few million years old. Those planets are still warm from their creation, and they therefore emit more radiation than planets in our solar system, which are 4.6 billion years old. Using this technique, astronomers have detected a few dozen planets bigger than Jupiter orbiting their stars.[8]

Scientists are actively working on technology that can block the light from a star to make it possible to see even fainter worlds. They use computers to accomplish this. Existing computer programs allow astronomers to subtract the light in a variety of clever ways. Scientists led by the Massachusetts Institute of Technology's Sara Seager are studying the possibility of sending up a set of two instruments

Sara **Seager**

(1971–)

For 20 years, astrophysicist Sara Seager has researched two important aspects of exoplanets. For one, she has simulated on computers what astronomers will see in the atmospheres of exoplanets once they have sufficiently advanced telescopes. Her second focus is to develop telescopes and instruments that will let astronomers actually see small rocky planets similar to Earth and study their gases. The upcoming generation of telescopes, she says, "has a shot at actually finding an Earth," and newer tools even farther in the future could find dozens of them. "We're the first generation ever in human history to soon have the capability to find signs of life on planets far away."[9]

Astronomy first interested Seager while she grew up in Toronto, Canada. She studied math and physics in college at the University of Toronto, and she graduated with her doctorate degree in astronomy from Harvard University in 1999. Seager has been at the Massachusetts Institute of Technology since 2007. In 2013, she was awarded a highly coveted MacArthur Fellowship, also known as a "genius grant," for her efforts in hunting new planets.

to fly separately in space: a telescope and a flower-shaped star shade that would lie thousands of miles away but be aligned just right to block the light from a star, allowing the telescope to spy an earthlike planet. The developers have tested a prototype in the lab. The idea may become reality in the future.

Early design drawings for WFIRST-AFTA show the coronagraph and sunshield that will make its observations possible.

Two Ways to Search

A space telescope slated for launch in the mid-2020s called WFIRST-AFTA will look at infrared light and hunt exoplanets in two ways. It will include instruments that work together as a coronagraph, a device that blocks starlight to make observations easier. The instruments make it easy to remove starlight and leave behind the light from a planet. Scientists say WFIRST-AFTA will be able to uncover exoplanets 1 billion times fainter than their stars.[10] The telescope would not be able to detect an Earth-sized planet orbiting a star the size of our sun, but it will be able to see larger planets the size of Jupiter and Saturn.

The same telescope will also be able to see planets orbiting their stars from farther out. However, this will require a very specific alignment: the star and exoplanet need to pass in front of a more distant star. Through a trick of gravity, the nearby star and its planet each magnify the light of the distant star, and astronomers see the brighter signals. This technique is called microlensing, and it can look for

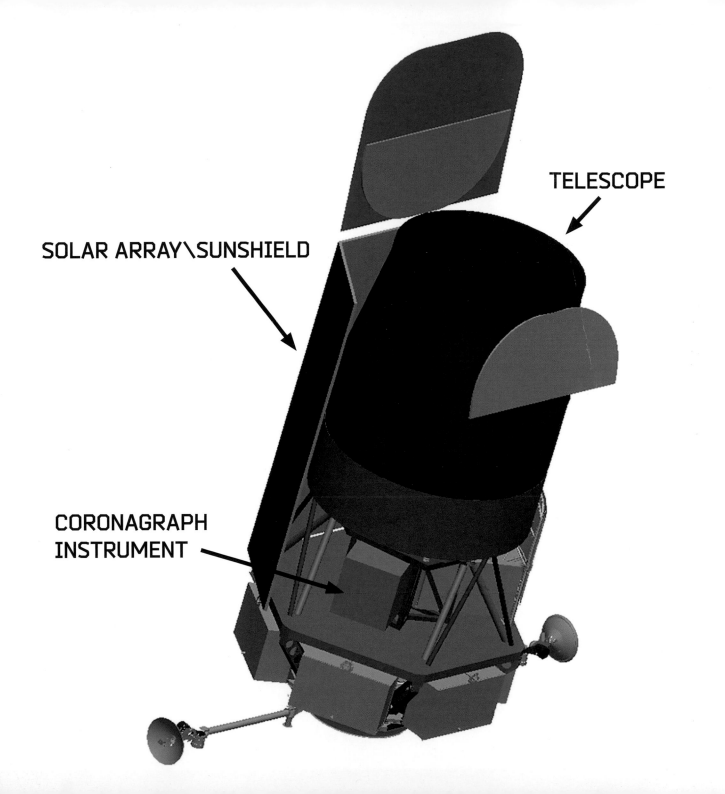

TELESCOPE

SOLAR ARRAY\SUNSHIELD

CORONAGRAPH
INSTRUMENT

planets far from their stars, 10 to 30 times farther out than Earth is from the sun. This is equivalent to the area where Uranus and Neptune orbit. Scientists have found a few dozen exoplanets using this technique, but they expect WFIRST-AFTA will detect thousands more.

Kepler's Successors

Several more cutting-edge space telescopes will look for exoplanets in the way Kepler did. NASA's Transiting Exoplanet Survey Satellite (TESS) will focus on nearby stars, those that live within a few hundred light-years of us. Most of these are stars a few thousand degrees cooler than our sun and are approximately half the size. For these stars' planets to be warm enough to hold liquid water, they need to orbit closer than Earth orbits the sun.

TESS is planned for a 2017 launch. It should be able to find thousands of exoplanets across the entire sky, including many relatively close to us. It will survey the nearest stars to the sun. Scientists will then pick several planets to study more closely. Astronomers will analyze their atmospheres, looking for signs of life.

Europe's Planetary Transits and Oscillations of stars (PLATO) spacecraft is another upcoming space telescope. It will use 34 separate small telescopes and associated detectors to survey 1 million stars across half the sky. PLATO's main goal is to find rocky planets similar in size to Earth orbiting their stars at the right distance to have liquid water on their surfaces. It will use the same technique as Kepler and TESS, watching for tiny dips in brightness as an exoplanet crosses its star.

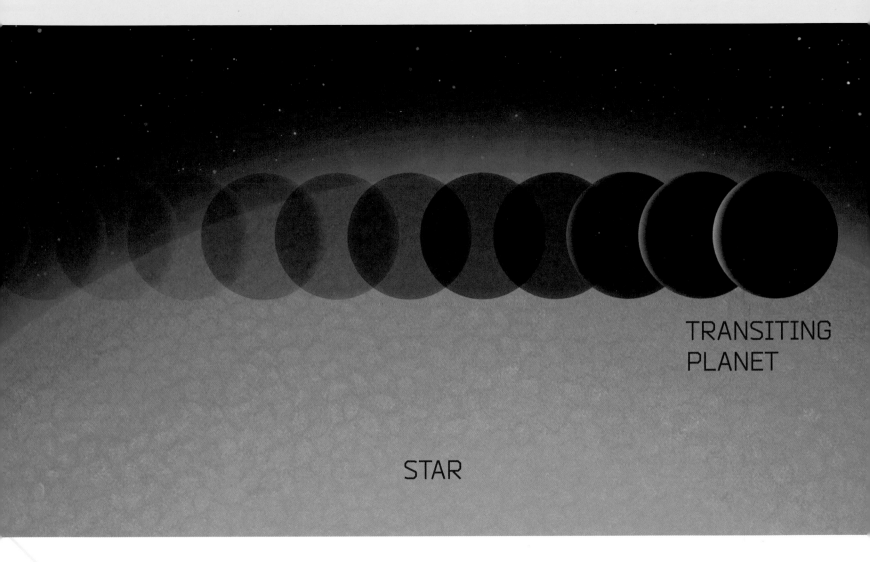

TRANSITING
PLANET

STAR

The transit method allows astronomers to find exoplanets by detecting the dip in brightness caused when the planet passes in front of its star.

Signals of Life

Earth hosts life, and these diverse life-forms alter our planet's atmosphere. They produce large amounts of oxygen, carbon dioxide, and methane, for example. Astronomers call these chemical gases biosignatures. As sunlight pours onto our planet, those chemical elements absorb specific colors of light. An alien civilization looking at Earth with advanced telescopes would be able to identify these elements by studying the planet's light. Looking for these same colors is how Earth's astronomers are searching for life on exoplanets.

Scientists can watch as an exoplanet passes in front of its star and study the world's atmosphere by how it filters starlight. So far they have done this only with large planets that could not host life. But soon they will start looking at smaller exoplanets that might have water. To find out if they are seeing signs of life, astronomers plug into a computer program what the atmosphere of an exoplanet should look like based on the world's size, mass, and the laws of chemistry and physics. If the filtered starlight suggests the presence of oxygen, carbon dioxide, and methane, then that world's atmosphere may signal the existence of life there.

The JWST will be astronomers' best tool to study infrared light. This enormous space telescope will have a much better chance than older tools of finding the signs of these important gases in the atmospheres of smaller exoplanets.

Listen for Messages

Some astronomers are looking for another form of evidence for life in space. They are listening for radio signals from the stars. Humans have been broadcasting radio signals for more than a century, and these messages have leaked into space. If other intelligent civilizations exist in our universe, they may have also been sending out radio signals.

Astronomers turn giant radio dishes toward stars that hold exoplanets, hoping to hear a message. So far, they have not heard any. It takes time for any radio message to get to us. Astronomers have only

been listening for such a message since 1960. Advanced radio telescopes, such as the Allen Telescope Array, have recently turned on. They can listen for fainter signals across a much larger area of sky.

Scientists are searching for planets that orbit within their star's habitable zone. Kepler-22b, approximately 620 light-years away, is one such planet.

Finding More Details

The past two decades have focused on finding exoplanets, but the next decade will see projects studying these worlds in more detail. The planets found so far are just the tip of the iceberg. The methods scientists have to detect worlds orbiting other stars can pick out only the biggest, brightest planets and those specially aligned to Earth. But they have learned most stars in our galaxy host at least one planet.

Even more exciting for the search for life elsewhere is that, on average, one in every five stars hosts an Earth-sized planet that could potentially have water on its surface. That does not mean those exoplanets are necessarily also rocky, as Earth is, and have oceans of water. After all, Mars is similar in size to Earth, and while scientists are confident the red planet has surface water, we have not yet found life on Mars.

The cutting-edge telescopes set to launch in the next few years will get us even closer, though, to the goal of finding more Earthlike planets that could potentially host life. The possibility that astronomers may soon discover life on other planets suggests we live in a special time in the intersection of astronomy science and technology.

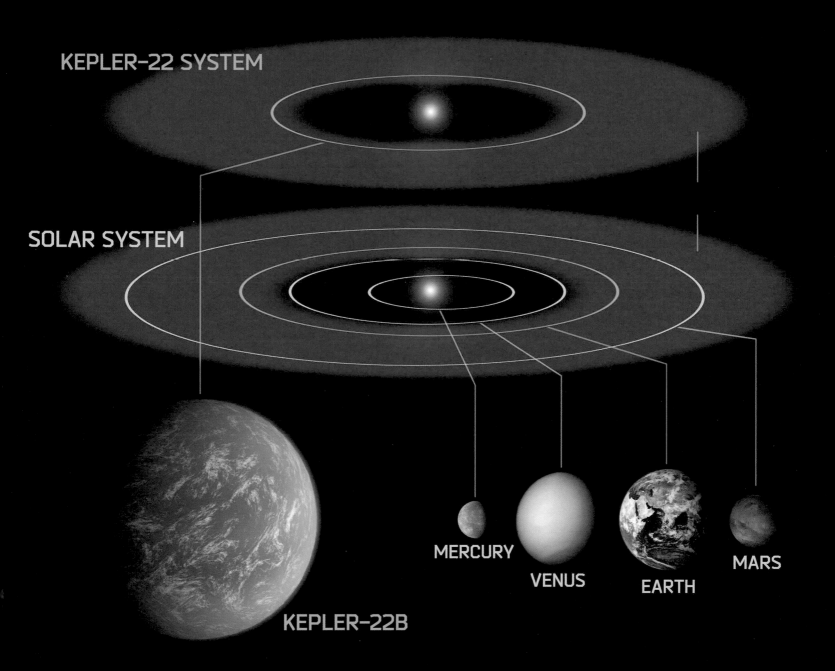

KEPLER-22 SYSTEM

SOLAR SYSTEM

KEPLER-22B

MERCURY

VENUS

EARTH

MARS

THE ENERGETIC
UNIVERSE

Black holes and exploding stars are key targets of high-energy astronomy. Scientists look to X rays and gamma rays, the types of light with the highest energies and smallest wavelengths, to study these exciting targets. The explosion at the end of a huge star's life, for example, generates energies humans cannot make in any laboratory on Earth. To study nature's extremes, scientists must look toward the sky.

To detect these energies, astronomers usually have to send telescopes above Earth's atmosphere. But they have also become very creative with developing new ways to search for high-energy signals without heading to space. They use the atmosphere and our planet itself to help in the search.

Black holes themselves are invisible, but they are surrounded by the swirling gases they draw in.

Black Holes

In astronomy, one force is of key importance: gravity. A black hole shows extreme gravity. It is a point in space that contains an enormous amount of mass. It can be the equivalent of cramming the mass of 30 suns into a tiny seed.[1] Its force of gravity is so strong even light that comes too close will be lost forever. This leaves black holes invisible to telescopes.

The universe has black holes of different sizes. Some form from stars at least 30 times the mass of our sun. These are stellar mass black holes. Some are millions to billions of times heavier. They live at the centers of large galaxies. These are supermassive black holes. Other black holes lie between these extremes. These are called intermediate mass black holes, and they have been the most difficult to find.

Scientists do not know exactly what happens inside a black hole. To learn about black holes, astronomers study how material moves near them. Watching stars at the very center of our galaxy showed astronomers a supermassive black hole must lie there. Two groups of astronomers using the best telescopes on Earth have tracked dozens of stars over the past 20 years. These stars have orbits around some unseen object, just as the planets in our solar system have orbits around the sun.

Andrea Ghez of the University of California, Los Angeles, led one team, and Reinhard Genzel of the Max Planck Institute in Germany led the other. Both groups calculated the unseen object is approximately 4 million times our sun's mass.[2] As far as astronomers know, any invisible cosmic object with that much mass crammed into an area the size of our solar system can only be a black hole.

Andrea **Ghez**
(1965–)

Andrea Ghez has spent more than 20 years watching stars circle an invisible and enormous black hole at our galaxy's center. Her research combines two of her main interests: black holes and imaging techniques. It also ties in two of her pursuits from her youth: puzzles and dance. "Doing astronomy," she says, is a field where "you get to try to sort out some of the biggest puzzles in the universe." And putting those pieces of those puzzles together can take a bit of choreography, Ghez adds.[4]

Her puzzle-solving interest led her to the Massachusetts Institute of Technology, where she got her degree in physics. She then moved to the California Institute of Technology and left in 1992 with her doctorate degree in physics. Two years later, she joined the faculty at the University of California, Los Angeles, just as the enormous Keck telescopes in Hawaii were starting to see cosmic light. Ghez has used those instruments, helping to improve the quality of their images and the detail they can see.

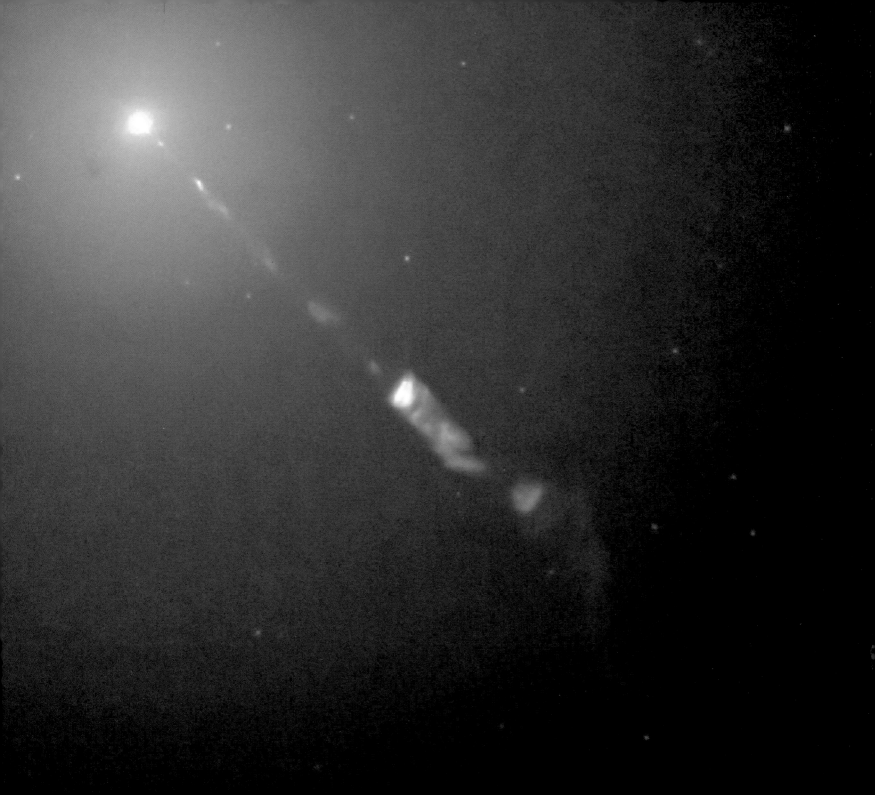

The Hubble Space Telescope captured an image of the supermassive black hole at the center of galaxy M87 shooting out a vast jet of particles.

While our galaxy's supermassive black hole is relatively inactive, scientists have found many galaxies with central black holes actively drawing in material. When stars, gas clouds, or dust particles come too close to the black hole, gravity pulls them in. Similar to water spiraling down a drain, the gas and dust circle the black hole and form a disk. As particles collide within the disc, the material generates heat and starts to glow. Sometimes the disk of material around the black hole can shoot out jets of light and matter. The resulting object is known as a quasar.

The glowing disks and jets are extremely bright, and astronomers can see them across vast distances in the universe. These galactic centers can outshine the billions of stars in their host galaxies. Astronomers study the X-ray light from those disks and the gamma-ray light from those jets to learn about black holes.

Even though astronomers have proven black holes exist, they still have not seen the edge of one. However, an upcoming project may be able to do so. The Event Horizon Telescope will use radio telescopes from across Earth as one large instrument. Astronomers will aim this worldwide observatory toward our galaxy's center in hopes of seeing a shadow—a place known as the event horizon, where light appears to stop as it gets pulled into the black hole.

New Views, New Discoveries

Some of the most exciting discoveries come when astronomers launch a telescope that can see a specific type of light for the first time. The NuSTAR observatory, launched in 2012, is the first telescope that can take photographs of extremely high-energy X rays.

In those images, astronomers found a huge amount of X ray light they had never seen before at our galaxy's center. They are not yet sure what is causing this glow. It could be small black holes or remnants left over after stars like our sun die.[5] It will likely take future observatories to find out what causes the light. The center of our galaxy is a unique place filled with many astronomical puzzles.

X-ray data, blue and green, from specialized telescopes can add an extra layer to composite images of celestial objects, including our sun.

Big Blasts in the Sky

When a big star ends its life, it does not go out with a whimper. Instead, it goes out in a bang. A star's explosion is a supernova, and it is so bright that for a few days it can outshine its galaxy. The process creates the heaviest elements found in nature. A star at least ten times the sun's mass burns through its fuel in millions of years, rather than in billions of years, like our sun. At its center, hydrogen atoms fuse together to make helium. The helium then makes carbon. More combinations produce heavier

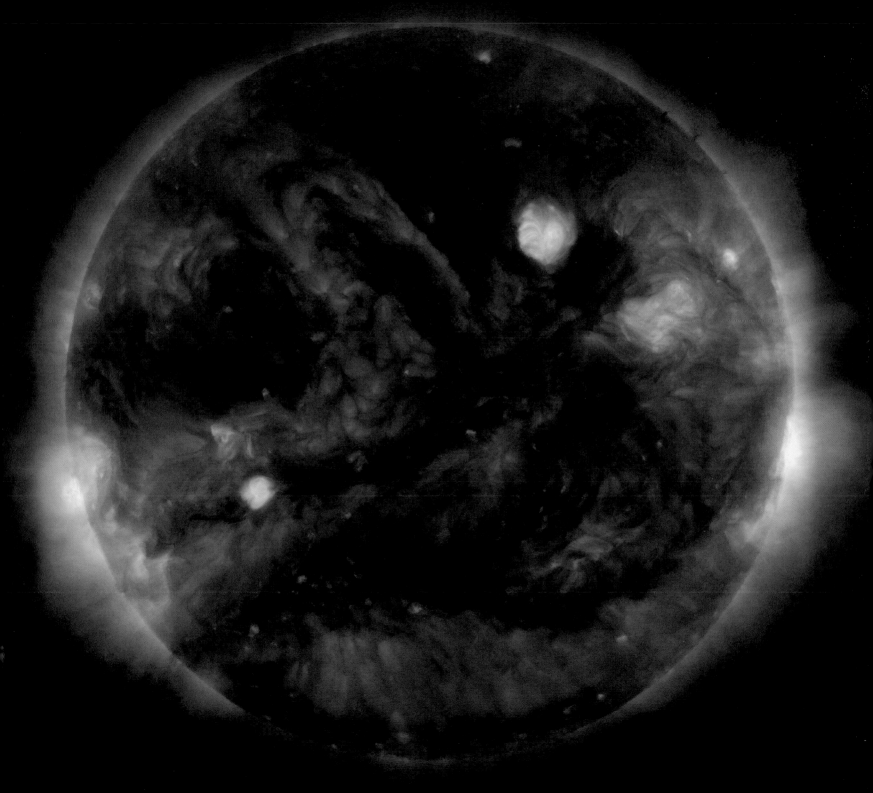

elements all the way up to iron. The core begins to collapse, then rebounds into an explosion that shoots most of the material into space. The collapsed core, known as a neutron star, is extremely dense. If the star was even larger, at least 30 times the sun's mass, astronomers think it will likely become a black hole after the explosion.[6]

The Crab Nebula is the remnant of a supernova that observers on Earth saw explode in 1054.

While astronomers know massive stars begin to collapse before they explode, they do not yet understand the details of supernova explosions. That is because they cannot see into the blasts. Instead, they must relay on observations of the material many years after it is thrown out. They combine those images with computer simulations.

Recent observations from NuSTAR of two explosion remnants have shown astronomers these stars do not explode evenly. Instead, these blasts are lopsided. Material sloshes around inside the star while different parts fall toward the center first.

The astronomers used NuSTAR to look at a specific color of X-ray light that comes from the element titanium. This chemical element is created during the supernova blast itself. They saw it shows up in clumps scattered across the remnant. No other telescope can image this color of light, so it was not possible to do this research until this new technology launched.

Cosmic Particles

The energy of a supernova's explosion can accelerate protons and electrons almost to the speed of light. Those particles then move through space as cosmic rays. Cosmic rays can collide with particles in our planet's atmosphere. They change into different particles and generate blue and ultraviolet light as they fall through to Earth. Scientists use telescopes to watch for these bursts of light. Detectors filled with water can capture the particles. Only recently have astronomers been able to turn these detectors into telescopes.

Evolving technology will improve the views researchers have of the sky in high-energy light. As is often the case in astronomy, scientists are likely to find that new methods uncover many more mysteries.

High-energy particles from the sun can create aurorae when they interact with Earth's atmosphere.

EIGHT

THE DARK
UNIVERSE

Everything we can see—all the stars, gas, dust, galaxies, planets, and everyday matter on Earth—make up only 4.9 percent of the entire universe.[1] The rest of the universe is dark. Every single point of light astronomers see through telescopes and other detectors represents less than 5 percent of the cosmos. A tremendous portion of the universe is cloaked in mystery.

Even though astronomers cannot see this invisible part of the cosmos, they know it exists by the way it affects galaxies, gases, and stars. Because of this invisibility, these unseen components of the universe are called dark matter and dark energy. Dark matter seems to have something in common with the material that we can see. It uses gravity to pull on stars and galaxies. But dark energy is a far greater mystery. Astronomers have determined dark matter and dark energy make up 25.9 and 69.2 percent of the universe, respectively.[2]

Astronomers detected dark matter and tinted it blue in photos from the Hubble Space Telescope to show its predicted location.

Gravity's Pull

Stars at the edges of galaxies zip around the centers of those galaxies more quickly than astronomers would expect. Some invisible force must be pulling on them. That force is gravity, and it comes from huge amounts of dark matter. Every galaxy sits within an enormous amount of this invisible material. Gravity also pulls together hundreds or thousands of galaxies into structures called galaxy clusters. Dark matter fills the space between the galaxies, holding them in the large cluster.

A 2005 supercomputer simulation created a model of the universe's dark matter distribution.

◢ Dark Matter Signal

Astronomers look to centers of galaxies for a signal from dark matter. These regions have more material crammed together than galaxies' outskirts do. That means there is a stronger gravitational pull to drag in more dark matter particles. Scientists think a collision between two of these particles would create an explosion that destroys the two particles and sends out a flash of gamma-ray light. Astronomers point their space-based gamma-ray telescopes to the centers of galaxies looking for this signal. They have found hints so far, but nothing certain.

Even though astronomers cannot see dark matter, they have creatively mapped it. They use gravity and one of its unique behaviors to do it. Sometimes scientists think of space as a stretchy fabric, like a trampoline planets, stars, and galaxies lay on. Any object in the universe warps that fabric; large objects such as galaxy clusters distort it more than less massive ones. Light that travels through space follows these warps, and its path bends.

If a bright galaxy is positioned on the other side of something very massive, its light will bend around the object as it journeys from the galaxy to our telescopes. Astronomers will see a distorted image of that galaxy. It can look similar to how a glass windowpane slightly warps the light streaming from a streetlamp. Astronomers study the warping of the light to learn where material lies within the

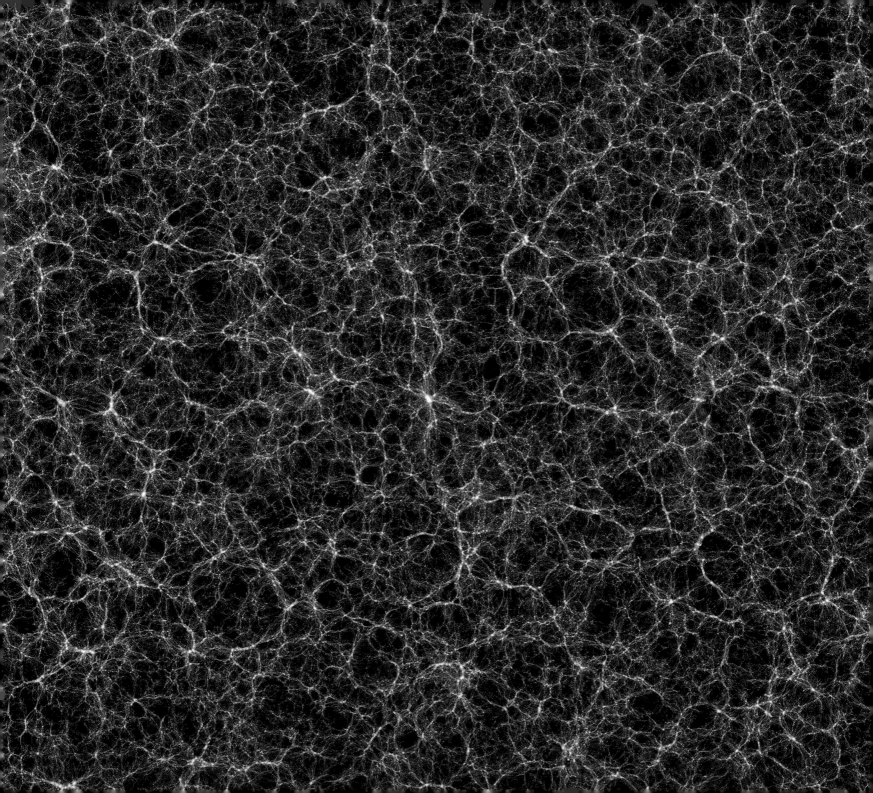

galaxy cluster. That is how they map the invisible dark matter.

Some telescopes that have recently started observing the sky, along with several starting soon, are making these maps. Astronomers use large telescopes with sensitive cameras that can take pictures of big parts of the sky in only a few days. The Dark Energy Camera on a telescope in Chile, for example, takes a few hundred images during each night, each covering 20 times more sky than the full moon.[3]

Seeing in the Dark

Scientists have not been able to determine what dark matter is made of. They know it is not made of the same building blocks as the visible universe, such as electrons, protons, and neutrons. They think it could be a type of particle not yet detected. It needs to be heavier than a proton, because it makes up so much of the universe. They have nicknamed these particles Weakly Interacting Massive Particles (WIMPs).

Scientists place detectors underground in hopes that when these dark matter particles fly through Earth, one of them will hit an atom in those detectors. That collision will send out a tiny signal. But no one has seen such a signal yet. Researchers keep building more sensitive detectors, though, with the expectation cutting-edge technology will help them find these mysterious particles.

Finding dark matter requires exotic, sensitive detectors.

They also expect the world's most powerful machine will create dark matter particles. The European Large Hadron Collider (LHC) slams together speeding protons, and these collisions create other particles. This technique has enabled physicists to detect many of the particles known to science today. If dark matter is made of WIMPs, this experiment may be able to generate them.

> ◢ **Nearby Forces**
>
> Even though most galaxies are moving
> away from Earth, pushed apart
> because of the mysterious dark
> energy, gravity overrides this force
> closer to home. Dark energy is not
> tearing apart our solar system or
> our galaxy. In fact, the gravity of our
> Milky Way and a neighboring enormous
> galaxy called the Andromeda Galaxy
> are too powerful for dark energy to
> split apart. Instead, the two galaxies
> are flying toward each other and will
> collide a few billion years in the future.

If scientists do not make dark matter particles at the LHC and do not detect them with their upcoming instruments, they will need to go back to the drawing board with their theories on what the mysterious material might actually be. The truth could be even more bizarre than we have imagined.

Repelling the Universe

Dark energy is even stranger than dark matter. Astronomers do not even think it is a material. Dark energy seems to be pushing everything away from everything else, so it acts against gravity.

Astronomers have known for decades the universe is getting bigger. They had expected it would reach a maximum size in the future. Then, the gravity of galaxies, gases, and dark matter would pull it back together into a single point, as it was before the big bang.

But in the late 1990s, when astronomers looked at faraway exploding stars, they uncovered a surprise. Their light was fainter than predicted, which means those stars were flying away from us faster than expected. Something was working against gravity, pushing the universe apart and speeding up its growth. Researchers know almost nothing about this dark energy.

The discovery was a huge surprise. Two teams of astronomers working across the globe from each other made the discovery at nearly the same time. This independent confirmation convinced many scientists the phenomenon was real. The astronomers who led the teams shared the 2011 Nobel Prize in Physics for their discovery.

To the Future

Whatever dark energy is, it also controls the future of the universe. Many billions of years from now, will all stars and galaxies be pushed so far apart from one another that no flickers of light will be seen in the night sky? Or will it speed up cosmic expansion so much it tears the fabric of space apart, ripping into pieces the remaining galaxies, stars, and planets?

While there is nothing we can do to change the ultimate fate of our universe, astronomers are using cutting-edge technology to learn more about dark energy. To do this, they need to study how the galaxies in our young universe grew. Telescopes and other experiments, such as the Dark Energy Camera and the upcoming space-based *Euclid* observatory, planned for launch in 2020, will begin revealing these dark secrets.

◢ Wrong Theory?

While most scientists are fairly certain dark matter and dark energy exist, others argue the generally accepted theory of gravity might be wrong instead. Gravity explains the motions of objects within the solar system perfectly, and it describes how stars fly around our galaxy's massive black hole. The theory of gravity has passed all the tests scientists have thrown at it. However, others argue gravity weakens at the largest scales, at distances of billions of light-years. This would explain why the universe's expansion is accelerating. If the theory of gravity turns out to be incomplete, it may mean dark matter does not exist after all.

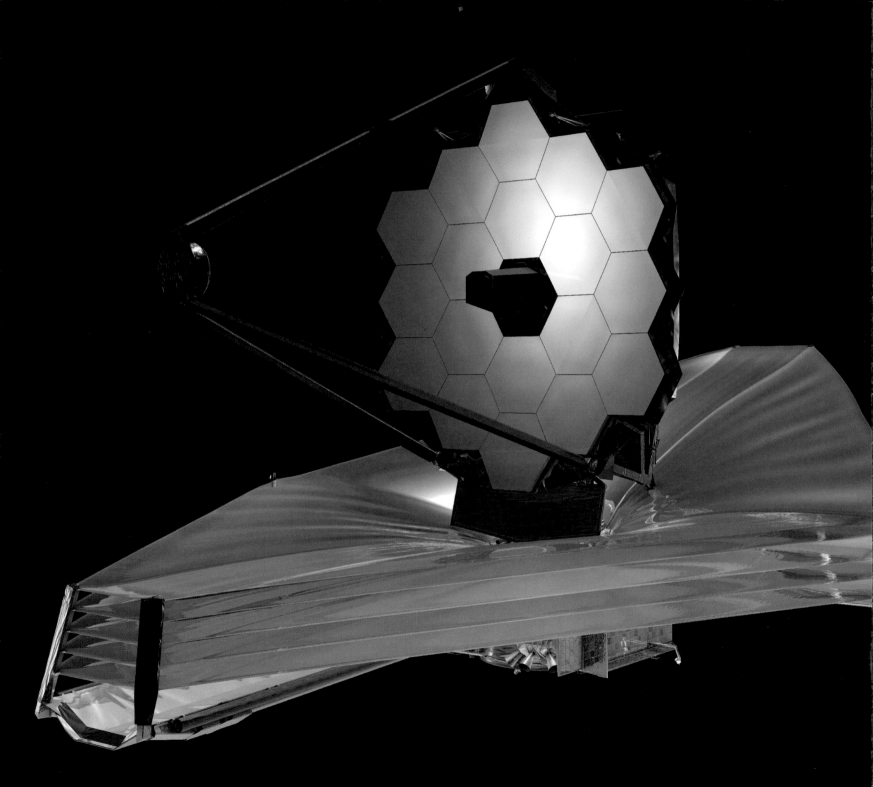

NINE

EXPLORING THE FUTURE

To answer astronomy's most exciting questions, scientists need bigger and better telescopes, both on Earth's surface and in space. They have started building the telescopes of the future. Planning and constructing these large, complex machines can take decades. The current generation of astronomers is using telescopes made by the previous generation. And today's astronomers are designing the telescopes for future astronomers. Cutting-edge telescopes will be able to see the dusty birthplaces of planets around other stars and clumps of baby stars in faraway galaxies.

Astronomy's most-anticipated space observatory, the JWST, has been in the works for decades. Once it is 930,000 miles (1.5 million km) away from Earth, it will give scientists the best views ever of the infrared sky.[1] The telescope's collector, 21.3 feet (6.5 m) wide, will see the faint light of some of the universe's first galaxies, bringing astronomers to the early history of our cosmos.[2]

The JWST is among the most-anticipated new tools for the next generation of astronomy.

The JWST has been an enormous project in terms of time, money, and expectations. The size of the project has delayed the progress of future large space observatories. Work is just starting on plans for the next major space telescope beyond the JWST.

The JWST is slated to launch aboard an Ariane 5 rocket.

Astronomers are hoping this future instrument will have a mirror between 33 and 39 feet (10 and 12 m) wide.[3] The telescope may be joined in space by a starshade 260 feet (80 m) wide to block light from stars, allowing the telescope to search directly for planets. This device would sit in space 100,000 miles (160,000 km) away from the telescope.[4]

This next-generation telescope has not yet gone through NASA's proposal process, which includes a study of the cost and tests of the technology. But scientists who have spent time focusing on this observatory idea believe it could be ready to propose to NASA in the mid-2020s. It would be considered for launch a decade later. Large space telescopes typically take approximately 20 years from the initial plans to launch.[5]

Similar to nearly all other observatories currently operating, this telescope would detect light—the usual messenger of astronomy. But there is other stuff flying through the cosmos scientists want to be able to see. These other messengers carry information about activities currently invisible to science. Instruments under development will open these new windows to the cosmos.

TELESCOPE SIZES

KEPLER TELESCOPE

HUBBLE SPACE TELESCOPE

JAMES WEBB SPACE TELESCOPE

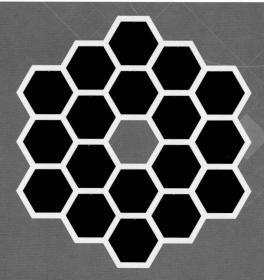

» The Kepler Telescope was launched in March 2009. It trails behind Earth in its orbit around the sun.

» The Hubble Space Telescope was launched in April 1990. It orbits Earth at an altitude of approximately 350 miles (560 km).

» The James Webb Space Telescope is slated for an October 2018 launch. It will fly to a point in space approximately 930,000 miles (1.5 million km) from Earth, directly opposite the sun.

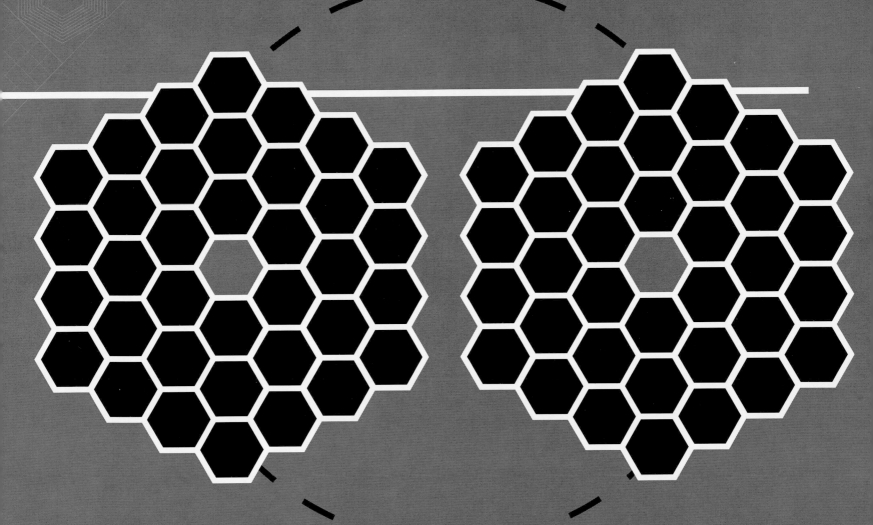

» The Keck Observatory is located atop Mauna Kea in Hawaii. The observatory's twin telescopes can work together as a single telescope with an enormous mirror.

Ghost Particles

Scientists first found ghostlike neutrinos coming from the sun in 1968. These particles have tiny amounts of mass, no electric charge, and rarely interact with other material. In fact, trillions of them pass through us every day without hitting a single atom.[6] That means scientists must set up enormous detectors to try to catch a few of these elusive particles.

Studying neutrinos often requires large, complex equipment, such as this enormous German spectrometer.

They have found neutrinos made at the heart of the sun, but what they really want to detect are neutrinos from the explosions of stars and other powerful events. Two detectors buried in Japan and the United States detected 19 neutrinos on February 23, 1987.[7] These particles came from a star that exploded in a nearby galaxy. This was the only time researchers found neutrinos coming from outside our solar system—until a few years ago.

Between 2010 and 2012, scientists detected dozens of neutrinos with energies a million times higher than the ones the supernova and the sun spit out. The scientists needed an enormous particle detector to catch these ghosts. That is precisely what IceCube, composed of thousands of sensors spread throughout a mass of pristine Antarctic ice, is. The scientists were unable to identify exactly where the neutrinos came from, but they knew the particles likely originated outside the Milky Way galaxy.

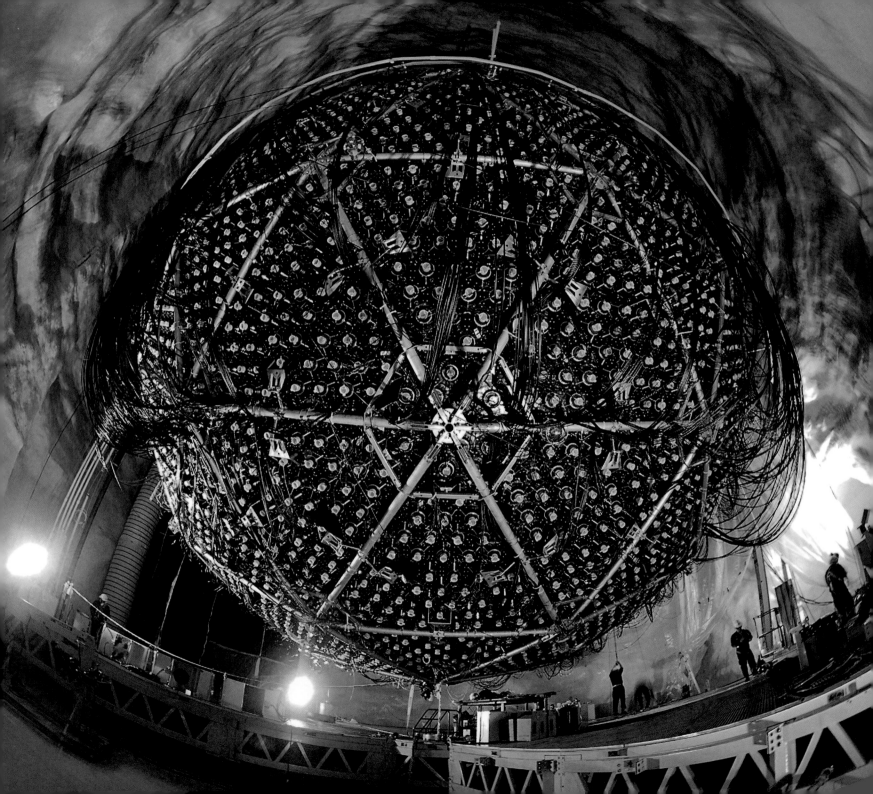

Neutrino observatories are located deep underground.

Neutrino particles are produced in the most intense environments and the biggest explosions in the universe. They carry information about those environments and explosions— regions and events light cannot probe. The huge blast produced when a black hole forms is one such explosion astronomers hope to study using neutrinos as messengers.

◄ **The X-Ray Sky**

In 2028, the European Space Agency will launch Athena+, the next large X-ray telescope. Astronomers will use the observatory to map what lies within hot, glowing gas found in deep space. Much of the universe's normal matter, made of electrons and protons, does not glow in visible light. Instead, it hides in this hot gas.

To detect more of these particles and find out where they are coming from, scientists need an even bigger detector. There are plans to expand the current Antarctic one to ten times its current size. With that larger volume, astronomers could detect ten times as many neutrinos and narrow down what is producing them.

Gravity Ripples

Scientists think gravity can move as waves through the fabric of space by compressing and stretching space. This is similar to how sound moves through air. Any fast-moving object would produce these gravitational waves. A planet orbiting a star would do it. So would a black hole on a collision course with another black hole. The second example would produce much stronger signals.

Astronomers at the European Space Agency want to launch an observatory known as LISA to look for these gravitational waves by the 2030s. Such a project will require detection technology that lies at the edge of what scientists are currently using.

In 2015, European scientists prepared to launch a mission called LISA Pathfinder to test these detection technologies. From 930,000 miles (1.5 million km) above Earth, the spacecraft will let two 1.8-inch (4.6 cm) metal cubes free-fall in gravity while keeping the spacecraft centered on the cubes.[10] The spacecraft will use thrusters while remaining perfectly still in relation to the cubes.

The LISA Pathfinder mission is an early step toward discovering gravitational waves.

This precise positioning comes from the need to carefully monitor how those cubes move in the observatory when it is operational. If a gravitational wave passes through space, it stretches and then shrinks space. The detectors onboard the spacecraft will detect any slight lengthening or shrinking of the space between the two test masses. On LISA Pathfinder, that distance is just 14 inches (35 cm). On the full-sized 2034 LISA mission, it will be millions of miles.[11] The changes the detectors look for are the size of an atom.

The first time scientists detect a gravitational wave will represent a major breakthrough in astronomy. Such a discovery will open a new view on the universe, giving new clues to how black holes live and die and revealing the earliest moments of the universe.

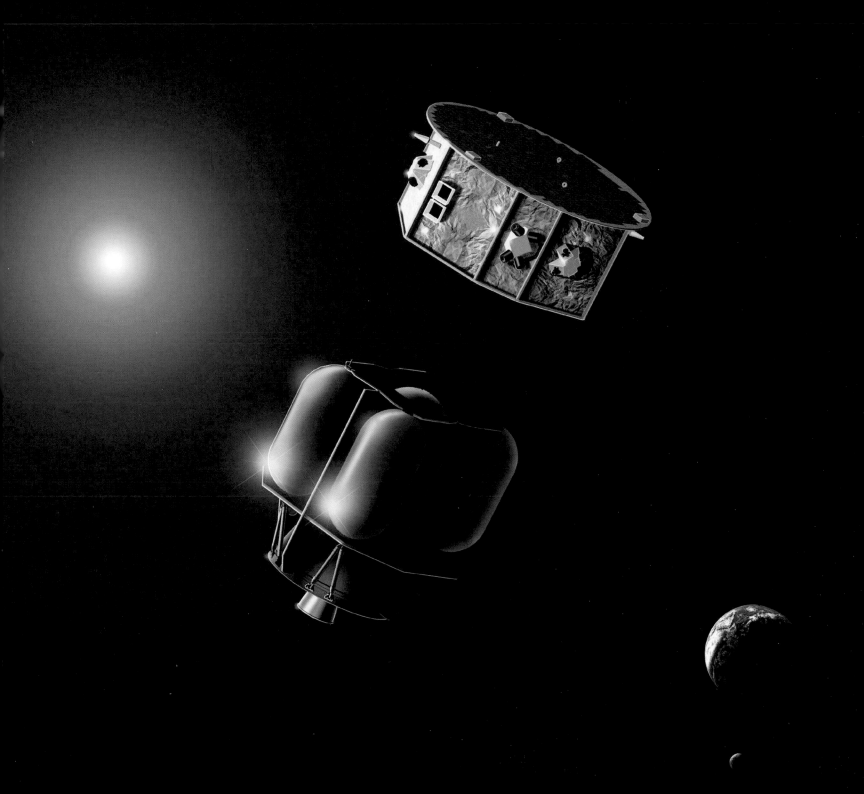

ESSENTIAL FACTS

Key Discoveries

» **Age of the Universe:** Our universe is 13.8 billion years old. It keeps getting bigger, and that expansion is speeding up.

» **Exoplanets:** By August 2015, scientists found more than 1,900 exoplanets.

» **The Milky Way's black hole:** A supermassive black hole with the mass of 4 million suns sits at the center of our galaxy.

Key Players

» **Andrea Ghez:** Andrea Ghez is an astrophysicist at the University of California, Los Angeles. She tracks stars around the invisible and enormous black hole at our galaxy's center.

» **Abraham Loeb:** Abraham Loeb is an astrophysicist at Harvard University. He studies the puzzles of the early universe to find ways to see the glow from the first stars and galaxies.

» **Sara Seager:** Sara Seager is an astrophysicist at the Massachusetts Institute of Technology. She researches the imprint biology has on planet atmospheres and develops tools that will let astronomers find those signs.

Key Tools and Technologies

» **Adaptive optics:** This telescope technology uses tiny motors on a mirror to offset the blurring effects of the atmosphere.

» **Spectroscopy:** Spectroscopy uses advanced prisms to spread out the light from an object and display its full range of colors, revealing what it is made of and how it moves through space.

» **Starshades:** A starshade is an instrument aligned just right to block the bright glare from a star and allow a telescope to detect the faint light from a planet orbiting that star.

» **Supercomputers:** A supercomputer is a powerful computer system that can perform trillions of calculations each second, allowing astronomers to run complex simulations tracking how the universe evolved.

Future Outlook

To answer astronomy's most exciting questions, scientists need bigger and better telescopes on Earth's surface and in space. These telescopes are time machines, collecting distant light from far reaches of the universe. Upcoming instruments will reach farther away and further back in time, letting astronomers probe closer to the cosmic beginning 13.8 billion years ago. Other observatories just starting up and still over the horizon will look for other types of messengers. These carry information about activities that are currently invisible, but which once detected will open new windows to the cosmos.

Quote

"We're the first generation ever in human history to soon have the capability to find signs of life on planets far away."

—*Sara Seager, Astrophysicist*

GLOSSARY

biosignature gas

A material produced by biological life-forms that astronomers seek to find in the atmospheres of planets orbiting other stars.

black hole

The densest object that exists; it has so much material crammed into a small space that nothing can escape its pull of gravity.

dark energy

A strange substance that acts against gravity and makes the universe expand faster.

dark matter

A mysterious type of matter that is not made of protons and electrons and does not reflect, emit, or absorb light; it makes up most of the universe's mass.

exoplanet

A planet orbiting a star other than the sun.

gamma ray

A form of light produced in the most energetic events in the universe, such as supernovas.

gravity

A fundamental force of nature; the pull between any two things in the universe.

Hubble's law

The idea that universe's expansion is moving distant galaxies away from us at faster speeds.

hydrogen

The most common chemical element in the universe, made of one proton and one electron.

microwave

A type of light with longer wavelengths than infrared.

nebula

A bright, indistinct object in the sky, sometimes composed of glowing dust or gas.

optical telescope

A telescope that makes observations in the visible-light portion of the electromagnetic spectrum.

orbit

The path an object takes around another object in space, held in place by the larger object's gravity.

supercomputer

An extremely powerful computer.

supermassive black hole

A black hole with a mass millions to billions of times that of our sun.

supernova

The explosion that marks the end of the life of the most massive stars.

terabyte

One trillion bytes, or one thousand gigabytes.

wavelength

The distance between two peaks of a wave.

ADDITIONAL RESOURCES

Selected Bibliography

"Exoplanets." Sara Seager, ed. Tucson, AZ: U of Arizona P, 2010. Print.

"James Webb Space Telescope." *NASA*. NASA, 2015. Web. 30 July 2015.

Further Readings

Trefil, James. *Space Atlas: Mapping the Universe and Beyond*. Washington, DC: National Geographic, 2012. Print.

Tyson, Neil deGrasse. *Death by Black Hole: And Other Cosmic Quandaries*. New York: Norton, 2014. Print.

Websites

To learn more about Cutting-Edge Science and Technology, visit **booklinks.abdopublishing.com**. These links are routinely monitored and updated to provide the most current information available.

For More Information

For more information on this subject, contact or visit the following organizations:

Adler Planetarium
1300 S Lake Shore Drive
Chicago, IL 60605
312-922-7827
http://www.adlerplanetarium.org

The Adler Planetarium has museum exhibits about historical telescopes, astronomy in culture, the timeline of our universe, and more. The planetarium also hosts many daily shows about astronomy topics for a wide range of ages.

Rose Center for Earth and Space, American Museum of Natural History
Central Park West at 79th Street
New York, NY 10024
212-769-5100
http://www.amnh.org/our-research/hayden-planetarium

The Rose Center for Earth and Space includes exhibits to explore the vast scales of the universe and learn about galaxies and stars. The museum also displays the largest meteorite ever found in the United States. The Hayden Planetarium, a 429-seat space theater, is also located at the site.

SOURCE NOTES

Chapter 1. Going the Distance

1. "How Many Solar Systems Are in Our Galaxy?" *NASA*. NASA, n.d. Web. 27 Aug. 2015.

2. "Fundamental Physics Constants." *National Institute of Standards and Technology*. National Institute of Standards and Technology, n.d. Web. 28 Aug. 2015.

3. Fraser Cain. "Distance to Andromeda." *Universe Today*. Universe Today, 11 May 2009. Web. 28 Aug. 2015.

4. Phil Plait. "The Universe Is 13.82 Billion Years Old." *Bad Astronomy*. Slate, 21 Mar. 2013. Web. 28 Aug. 2015.

5. Mario De Leo Winkler. "The Farthest Object in the Universe." *Huff Post Science*. Huffington Post, 15 July 2015. Web. 28 Aug. 2015.

6. "Confirmed Planets." *NASA Exoplanet Archive*. NASA Exoplanet Science Institute, n.d. Web. 28 Aug. 2015.

7. Ken Croswell. "Far Out: The Most Distant Star in the Milky Way." *Scientific American*. Scientific American, 11 Aug. 2014. Web. 28 Aug. 2015.

8. Ashley P. Taylor. "Scientists Detect 12-Billion-Year-Old Supernova, the Oldest Yet Observed." *Discover*. Discover, 6 Nov. 2012. Web. 31 Aug. 2015.

9. "Hubble Essentials." *Hubble Site*. Hubble Site, n.d. Web. 28 Aug. 2015.

10. "Keck Observatory." *W. M. Keck Observatory*. W. M. Keck Observatory, 2014. Web. 28 Aug. 2015.

11. "About the James Webb Space Telescope." *James Webb Space Telescope*. NASA, n.d. Web. 28 Aug. 2015.

12. "Frequently Asked Questions." *James Webb Space Telescope*. NASA, n.d. Web. 28 Aug. 2015.

13. "Hubble's Deepest View of the Universe Unveils Bewildering Galaxies across Billions of Years." *Hubble Site*. Hubble Site, 15 Jan. 1996. Web. 28 Aug. 2015.

14. "Hubble Goes to the eXtreme to Assemble Farthest-Ever View of the Universe." *Hubble Space Telescope*. NASA, 25 Sept. 2012. Web. 28 Aug. 2015.

15. Elizabeth Howell. "How Many Galaxies Are There?" *Space.com*. Space.com, 1 Apr. 2014. Web. 31 Aug. 2015.

16. "Planck Reveals the Dynamic Side of the Universe." *Phys.Org*. Phys.org, 11 Feb. 2015. Web. 28 Aug. 2015.

Chapter 2. Beginning a Cosmic Exploration

1. "The Telescope." *The Galileo Project*. Rice University, 1995. Web. 31 Aug. 2015.

2. "Cepheid Variable Stars & Distance Determination." *Australia Telescope National Facility*. Australia Telescope National Facility, n.d. Web. 31 Aug. 2015.

3. "1923: Other Galaxies Exist." *Telescopes from the Ground Up*. Space Telescope Science Institute, n.d. Web. 31 Aug. 2015.

4. "From Our Galaxy to Island Universes." *Ideas of Cosmology*. American Institute of Physics, 2015. Web. 31 Aug. 2015.

5. Fraser Cain. "Distance to Andromeda." *Universe Today*. Universe Today, 11 May 2009. Web. 28 Aug. 2015.

Chapter 3. The Tools of Astronomy

1. "SOFIA Overview." *SOFIA*. NASA, 30 July 2015. Web. 31 Aug. 2015.

2. "Aircraft Facts." *SOFIA*. SOFIA, n.d. Web. 31 Aug. 2015.

3. "E-ELT Telescope Design." *European Southern Observatory*. European Southern Observatory, 23 Aug. 2012. Web. 31 Aug. 2015.

4. "World's Most Advanced Mirror for Giant Telescope Completed." *UA Science Mirror Lab*. University of Arizona, 2012. Web. 31 Aug. 2015.

5. "Interferometry." *ALMA*. ALMA, n.d. Web. 31 Aug. 2015.

6. "The Location of the SKA." *Square Kilometer Array*. Square Kilometer Array, 2015. Web. 31 Aug. 2015.

7. "Instrumentation." *NuSTAR*. NuSTAR, n.d. Web. 31 Aug. 2015.

8. "Falcon 9." *SpaceX*. SpaceX, 2015. Web. 31 Aug. 2015.

9. "Vital Facts." *James Webb Space Telescope*. James Webb Space Telescope, n.d. Web. 31 Aug. 2015.

10. "The Primary Mirror." *James Webb Space Telescope*. James Webb Space Telescope, n.d. Web. 31 Aug. 2015.

11. Ghez, Andrea. Personal interview. 24 June 2015.

SOURCE NOTES CONTINUED

Chapter 4. Simulating the Universe

1. "CDC 6600's Five Year Reign." *Computer History Museum*. Computer History Museum, 2015. Web. 31 Aug. 2015.

2. "November 2014." *Top 500*. Top 500, 2015. Web. 31 Aug. 2015.

3. "Victor Blanco 4-m Telescope." *Cerro Tololo Inter-American Observatory*. NOAO, n.d. Web. 31 Aug. 2015.

4. "About." *Large Synoptic Survey Telescope*. LSST, n.d. Web. 31 Aug. 2015.

5. "LSST General Public FAQs." *Large Synoptic Survey Telescope*. LSST, n.d. Web. 31 Aug. 2015.

6. Peter Dizikes. "The Universe in a Cube." *MIT News*. MIT, 7 May 2014. Web. 31 Aug. 2015.

Chapter 5. The Universe's Beginning

1. Nola Taylor Redd. "How Old Is the Universe?" *Space.com*. Space. com, 20 Dec. 2013. Web. 31 Aug. 2015.

2. "Tests of Big Bang: The CMB." *Universe 101*. NASA, 12 May 2015. Web. 31 Aug. 2015.

3. Lawrence M. Krauss. "Viewpoint: Peering Back to the Beginning of Time." *Physics*. American Physical Society, 19 June 2014. Web. 31 Aug. 2015.

Chapter 6. Planets around Other Stars

1. "Extrasolar Planets." *Hubble 25*. NASA, 11 Dec. 2014. Web. 31 Aug. 2015.

2. "NASA's Kepler Marks 1,000th Exoplanet Discovery." *Jet Propulsion Laboratory*. NASA, 6 Jan. 2015. Web. 31 Aug. 2015.

3. "Mars Fact Sheet." *NASA*. NASA, 13 Aug. 2015. Web. 31 Aug. 2015.

4. Clara Moskowitz. "'Habitable Zone' for Alien Planets, and Possibly Life, Redefined." *Space.com*. Space.com, 29 Jan. 2013. Web. 31 Aug. 2015.

5. "Mars Fact Sheet." *NASA*. NASA, 13 Aug. 2015. Web. 31 Aug. 2015.

6. Sara Seager. "Is There Life Out There?" *MIT*. MIT, 2009. Web. 31 Aug. 2015.

7. "Starshade." *Northrop Grumman*. Northrop Grumman, 2014. Web. 31 Aug. 2015.

8. "Catalog." *Exoplanet.eu*. Exoplanet.eu, 2015. Web. 31 Aug. 2015.

9. Seager, Sara. Personal interview. 24 June 2015.

10. N. Jeremy Kasdin. "Exoplanet Imaging Science with the WFIRST Coronagraph." *WFIRST*. AAS Conference, 2015. Web. 31 Aug. 2015.

Chapter 7. The Energetic Universe

1. Dave Rothstein. "What Is the Density of a Black Hole?" *Ask an Astronomer*. Cornell, 27 June 2015. Web. 31 Aug. 2015.

2. Liz Kruesi. "How We Know Black Holes Exist." *Astronomy Magazine*. Astronomy Magazine, April 2012. Web. 31 Aug. 2015.

3. Frank Heile. "What Would the Death of a Black Hole Look Like?" *Quora*. Slate, 12 Nov. 2013. Web. 7 Oct. 2015.

4. Ghez, Andrea. Personal interview. 24 June 2015.

5. "NASA's NuSTAR Captures Possible 'Screams' from Zombie Stars." *NuSTAR*. NuSTAR, 29 Apr. 2015. Web. 31 Aug. 2015.

6. Liz Kruesi. "How We Know Black Holes Exist." *Astronomy Magazine*. Astronomy Magazine, April 2012. Web. 31 Aug. 2015.

7. "Frequently Asked Questions." *Hubble Site*. Hubble Site, n.d. Web. 31 Aug. 2015.

Chapter 8. The Dark Universe

1. "Planck Reveals the Dynamic Side of the Universe." *CNES*. CNES, 5 Feb. 2015. Web. 31 Aug. 2015.

2. Ibid.

3. "DECam." *The Dark Energy Survey*. The Dark Energy Survey, n.d. Web. 31 Aug. 2015.

Chapter 9. Exploring the Future

1. "About JWST's Orbit." *James Webb Space Telescope*. James Webb Space Telescope, n.d. Web. 31 Aug. 2015.

2. "First Light & Reionization." *James Webb Space Telescope*. James Webb Space Telescope, n.d. Web. 31 Aug. 2015.

3. "Beyond JWST: Technology Path to a High Definition Space Telescope." *AURA*. AAS, Jan. 2015. Web. 31 Aug. 2015.

4. Ibid.

5. Julianne Dalcanton. "UVOIR Space Astronomy Beyond the 2020's." *AURA*. AAS, 2015. Web. 31 Aug. 2015.

6. "Neutrino Physics." *Berkeley Center for Theoretical Physics*. Berkeley, n.d. Web. 31 Aug. 2015.

7. Malcolm W. Browne. "Particles From Stellar Explosion Are Detected." *New York Times*. New York Times, 11 Mar. 1987. Web. 31 Aug. 2015.

8. "People." *James Webb Space Telescope*. James Webb Space Telescope, n.d. Web. 31 Aug. 2015.

9. "Introduction: The Large Hadron Collider." *New Scientist*. New Scientist, 27 Aug. 2008. Web. 31 Aug. 2015.

10. "LISA Pathfinder." *Space Science*. ESA, 6 June 2013. Web. 31 Aug. 2015.

11. Ibid.

INDEX

About the Author

Liz Kruesi found her love of astronomy and dark skies at a young age, during family trips to the Adirondack Mountains in upstate New York. As her fascination with observational astronomy grew, the Hubble Space Telescope began capturing incredible portraits of the universe. Her interest in astronomy led her to earn her bachelor's degree in physics (with a minor in English) from Lawrence University in Appleton, Wisconsin. She also studied graduate astrophysics at Iowa State University in Ames. Since then, Liz has written about astronomy, space, and physics. She loves to tell the stories of our beautiful universe. She is a contributing editor of *Astronomy* magazine, where she also worked for more than seven years. Her articles have also appeared in *Discover* magazine, *New Scientist*, and others. She has also won a science writing award from the American Astronomical Society for an article she wrote about black holes. When not talking and writing about science, Liz kayaks, cooks, or spends time with her husband and their adopted border collie mix, Kara.